D0048634

Frank McDonald is Environment Correspondent of *The Irish Times* and author of *The Destruction of Dublin*, published in 1985 by Gill and Macmillan. In 1979, he won the award for outstanding work in Irish journalism for a series entitled *Dublin - What Went Wrong?* He also received a Lord Mayor's Millennium Award in 1988 for his work in making the public more aware of the architecture of the city.

SAVING THE CITY

HOW TO HALT THE DESTRUCTION OF **DUBLIN**

By Frank McDonald

TOMAR PUBLISHING LTD.

Published by
Tomar Publishing Ltd.
Bloom House,
78 Eccles Street,
Dublin 7.

First published 1989
Copyright © Frank McDonald 1989
ISBN 1 871793 03 3

Design and typography by
The Cloake Nugent Design Partnership.

A completely Irish produced book
Cover photograph and design by
Nicholas Cloake Ad. Dip. V.C.
Mary Lohan A.N.C.A.D.

In memory of Desmond MacWeeney,
who fought many a quiet battle to save the city.

ACKNOWLEDGEMENTS

I had not intended writing this book *(The Destruction of Dublin* was more than enough), and I wouldn't have written it but for the repeated urgings of P.J. Drudy. To him, I owe a considerable debt - both for the genesis of *Saving the City* and for his many helpful comments on the text as it developed.

Originally, the intention was to update the Dublin Crisis Conference *Manifesto for the City*, including references to the various events of importance which had taken place in the city since 1985, when The *Destruction of Dublin* was published. But like the universe, it kept on expanding to take in a plethora of material and, in the process was transformed from a pamphlet into a book.

Others need to be thanked. Conor Brady, the editor of *The Irish Times,* had no hesitation in giving me the freedom to re-use some material from articles I have written for the paper, particularly a series entitled "Living in the City", published in February 1989. And my immediate superior, news editor Eugene McEldowney, was always accommodating (well, almost) to my requests for time off to pursue it.

My colleague Pat Langan, who has a great feeling for Dublin himself, took many of the photographs on a whizz around the city one sunny summer's day. The bulk of the remaining pictures were culled from the files of *The Irish Times* or taken by colleague Peter Thursfield in 1984 for *The Destruction of Dublin.*

I am also grateful to Colin Scudds for his permission to use the two photographs of Cornmarket, 70 years apart, which provide the most devastating evidence I've seen for the havoc wreaked on Dublin, and to John O'Regan, of Gandon Editions, for his expert advice at an early stage - especially on the mechanics of it all.

Tom Breen and Padraig Yeates, of Tomar Publishing, took the project on board with amazing speed and I had to work hard trying to keep up with them. Felicity Hogan and Tom O'Connell provided the legal advice to lead us through what has become a libel minefield. I also want to thank Bob Geldof for writing the introduction (and his sisters Lynn and Cleo for egging him on), Tony Reddy for reading the typescript, Ian Lumley for his numerous suggestions, and Eamonn Slater for putting up with it all - again.

The book is dedicated to Desmond MacWeeney, who was assistant secretary of An Taisce from 1967 until his death in October 1982. These were crucial years for Dublin and, despite his advanced age, Desmond tried as best he could to keep up with what was happening and to ensure that the sane voice of conservation was heard, even it it was rarely heeded. Would that there were many more prepared to undertake this often thankless task.

Frank McDonald,
Dublin, August 1989.

INTRODUCTION

It is alarming that only five years after Frank McDonald's last despair inducing book, he finds it necessary to shock us into renewed outrage over the wilful destruction of our city. Dublin is being savaged, with an almost methodical municipal vandalism.

With distance perhaps one sees it more clearly, for it is a terrible savagery perpetrated by the greedy, the corrupt, the stupid, the uninspired, the mediocre, the cheap, the tawdry, the vulgar - but mainly the indifferent. Its tool is greed, its logic progress. But progress towards what?

Is their idea of progress the simple reduction of every political and philosophical ideal to the single word "more". Or is it done in the name of the other great totem of our age, the god Development, and its attendant illusion that given a facade of prosperity and modernism, Ireland could be up there with the big boys. Perhaps it's even simpler than all that, maybe it's just the cack-handed reaction of old buffers, still clinging to the tattered shreds of their long-discredited notions of social engineering.

Whatever their logic and reasons Dublin remains (just about) a small jewel on the western edge of an indifferent Europe. The jewel is, sadly, increasingly and almost irreparably flawed. We invent spurious millennia to celebrate a city we seem to hold in contempt or at least no longer to care about. A 1,000 years has been invested in building a city we can destroy in thirty years.

Those inhabitants so often celebrated in book, song or play we shift to unspeakably inhuman suburban islands where they remain stranded without jobs, services or community. The soulless void remaining is left to the ravages and incoherence of development or is simply left empty to become another dangerous wasteland.

Those streets we eulogise in anniversaries to artists we once exiled, banned and ridiculed, we now compound and make more ridiculous by prissy pedestrianisation and the erection of garish and inappropriate statuary, neatly obliterating the very characters being celebrated while the traffic grows and new roads are mooted that will eradicate or despoil whole areas of town and bay.

Those squares we boast of as unique in their pristine geometric eloquence we save our greatest contempt for. By plundering one side of four we cut off a limb and leave the rest to slowly and inevitably die of a massive haemor-

rhage, while we turn away in cowardly embarrassment as from a flawless beauty whose face is now irredeemably scarred.

I am aware that there is a recognition of past failure, but where are the remedies to those failures? Where are the lessons learned? As this book points out the damage gets worse and the pressure for further "development" is quantum times greater with, if anything, more cowboys involved than ever before. Where is the informed opinion? Where are the overall plans that understand what Dublin is and where it should go?

I have seen the Docklands schemes and some newer housing developments, but they are scattered and really not all that impressive. And if they are meant to somehow substitute for something like the destruction, or "facadism", of Bachelors Walk then it is no alternative or substitution.

So what of the responsibilities of the builders and the architects of Ireland? What of their skill, what of their pride? Stephenson and Scott have left behind them the most preposterous and obvious of our new structures. But, God help us, they apparently represent the pinnacle of Irish architectural achievement.

At least Stephenson's bunkers accurately represent the impenetrable arrogance and contempt of civic authority in Dublin for the wishes of its citizens.

The city dies if no-one lives there. At night, wind, waste and danger occupy uninhabited streets that once rang with real life, and soon the urban organism collapses and dies, as will any living thing once its heart has been removed.

Frank McDonald has now written two books which devastatingly tell how, why, and by whose hand this dying has occurred. They are not protest books. They are researched impeccably, they are crafted thoroughly, they are written with passion and argued with urgency. If only for the fact that for so long his voice has been one of the few media voices raised against the systematic destruction of his city, one should read him. If only for the fact that he remains a permanent thorn in the fat arse of municipal pretension, one should support him.

McDonald does not argue for a return to some mythical Arcadian notion of the past, nor a retention of the present in municipal urban aspic. He also absolutely rejects the fetishism of the "new" for its own sake, while supporting good modern architecture in the right places. This is a sane man's plea for the idea of a city and the buildings and people who give it its specific and genuinely unique atmosphere. It is the book of a man who loves where he lives and is now very afraid that "they" will take it away from him.

He argues for the steady and stately advance of Dublin looking back and around at what it is and has been. For we can no longer count on the future of Dublin being an extension of its past and if this is the case the very thing which makes us Dubliners will have disappeared. We may not simply be looking at the demise of a city but of an entire attitude to life.

It is a legendary "modus operandi et vivendi" giving this city an importance, respect and mystique out of all proportion to its size. What will replace it? No-one seems to know or much care, but at least with these books we will know who was responsible - besides ourselves.

Bob Geldof
August 1st 1989

Contents

Chapter One	*Perceptions of the City.*	Page 15
Chapter Two	*A Question of Transport.*	Page 33
Chapter Three	*Containing Suburban Sprawl.*	Page 73
Chapter Four	*Stopping the Rot.*	Page 99
Chapter Five	*What is to be done.*	Page 125
Appendix One	*Dublin City Council's roll-call votes on crucial road schemes.*	Page 173
Appendix Two	*Resolution of the Dublin Crisis Conference, adopted unanimously at the conclusion of the three-day conference in the Synod Hall, Christchurch Place, in February 1986.*	Page 174
Appendix Three	*Conclusion of the RIAI's Millennium Conference-"Dublin: A Positive Strategy" - October, 1988.*	Page 176
Appendix Four	*An Extract from the National Development Plan indicating the Government's priorities for the Dublin sub-region.*	Page 177
Appendix Five	*The Citizens' Alternative Plan for Dublin.*	Page 178
Appendix Six	*Extract from the Fianna Fail - Progressive Democrats' Programme for Government, published in July 1989*	Page 184
Select Bibliography		Page 185
Index		Page 186

1

Perceptions of the City

Stand on any of the canal bridges between five and six o'clock in the evening and you'll see very clearly what has happened to Dublin. Every crossing is jammed with cars as the suburban commuters head for home, their rear red lights almost a symbol of how the middle classes have abandoned the city over the past 150 years - ever since Dublin first had a middle class, in fact.

Dublin has become a suburban city. In 1926, when it was a compact sort of place, nearly two-thirds of Dubliners lived in what we now call the inner city - the 4,000 acres or so locked in between the Grand Canal, the Royal Canal and the North Circular Road. Now it's less than one in twelve. Indeed, over the past 25 years, the population of the city's historic core has been cut in half - from 160,000 to just 80,000. And if present trends continue unchecked, it will fall even further, to just 50,000 by the year 2000. If the main residential areas in the western half of the inner city area, in the vicinity of the North and South Circular roads, are excluded from the calculation, it would show that the heart of Dublin has been almost stripped bare of the population that once sustained it. Is it any wonder, therefore, that the area is littered with large and small derelict sites, many of them now in use as parking lots to accommodate the daily flood of commuters in their cars?

Many reasons may be offered to explain this flight from the city to the suburbs. First, there was the pervasive influence of the Garden City ideal, offering people the prospect of fresh air, modern homes and generous gardens front and back. Then, there was the relentless slum clearance programme pursued by Dublin Corporation from the 1920s onwards. And, more recently, there was a massive haemhorrage in the housing stock itself with the loss - through conversion or demolition - of hundreds, even thousands, of houses to the office sector. The southside Georgian area is now so overwhelmed by offices that the streets are virtually dead after dark. Even the floodlighting of houses in Merrion Square seems slightly pathetic - an attempt, perhaps, to compensate for the fact that there is no light coming from within. And in the more deprived areas of the inner city, though the tenements of Sean O'Casey's time may be gone, the powerful image of squalor lives on in the weed-strewn derelict sites, the terraces of tumbledown buildings and the bleak blocks of Corporation flats.

The state of the inner city was summed up by the Government- appointed consultants who carried out a study of Dublin with a view to maximising aid from the EC Structural Funds. "Side by side with prosperity and affluence are to be found poverty, decay and dereliction in twilight areas adjoining the Central Business District [CBD]. The rapid growth of the city in peripheral areas has been paralleled by decline at its core. Failure to resolve conflicting pressures and demands, together with a lack of investment in physical and social infrastructure in the Inner City, has contributed to the nature and extent of the problem which now exists". The perception of urban decline is reinforced by the first glimpse you see of the inner city at many of the canal bridges - the "gates" which mark the transition from the suburbs. At Binns Bridge, between Drumcondra and Dorset Street, there is a row of single-storey shack-like shops. At Harold's Cross bridge, there is a scrapyard, a fuel depot, a used car lot and a back-street abbatoir. And at Charlemont Street bridge, on the way in from Ranelagh, there is nothing more than a wilderness with a few disjointed office blocks in the distance. It all adds up to a foreboding picture of decay, not exactly the kind of place you would want to live in.

Not everyone would see it that way. Frank Convery, professor of environmental studies at University College Dublin, points out that there is a "huge perception gap" between the middle and lower classes in terms of how they view the inner city. "Working class Dubliners would give their eye-teeth for a Corporation house in the city and, for every house that's built, there are literally dozens of families who want it", he says. "A lot of this has to do with family ties and the tremendous community loyalty you find in the inner city - the kind of spirit which brings people back from Clondalkin, even if it's only to shop in Meath Street on a Saturday afternoon. You just don't find that in, say, Castleknock or Dundrum". For the middle classes, however, the suburbs are so much more attractive than the inner city. There are good houses, good schools, convenient shopping centres and, as one leading chartered surveyor put it, "you don't have to worry about your children walking home after 11 o'clock at night". Crime is not a major problem, unlike in the inner city where statistics show that nearly two-thirds of all the indictable crimes in the Corporation area are committed. For suburbanites, it comes as no surprise that the inner city shops are shuttered, some with steel bars stuck in the ground to deter frontal assaults by joyriders.

This is what lies behind the current round of Northsider jokes, like the one which goes: "What do you call a Northsider wearing a suit and tie?" Answer: "The Accused". The gut feeling is that the inner city - especially the northside - is a dangerous place, where you couldn't park a car with any degree of security and, if you owned a property there, it would need to be wired for alarms with a direct line to Store Street Garda Station. Indeed, when I asked one Dublin planner why he lived 20 miles away rather than in the heart of the city, he replied - only half-jokingly - "I haven't got enough locks". Obviously, there is a middle class dread in Dublin of being close to the poor and what are seen as the "criminal classes"; that helps to explain why the city is among the most socially segregated in Europe. But according to Arthur Gibney, president of the Royal Institute of the Architects of Ireland, Dublin may also be losing its urban sensibilities as a result of being over-run by "the inhabitants of its hinterland" (a polite way of saying Culchies), with their "provincial values", as well as the general exodus from the city to the suburbs. "After two generations of non-city living, the myth and memory of city life has nearly disappeared", he complains.

Indeed, the suburbs might even be seen as a purgatorial half-way house between the hell of city life and the heavenly ideal of so many of Ireland's *nouveau riche* - a Southfork-style *palazzo* plonked in the middle of the countryside. This greenfield mentality is also reflected in the location of Industrial Development Authority "advance factories", industrial estates and "office parks". It may be seen at work, too, in the closure of inner city schools and hospitals and their replacement by new facilities in the suburbs, and there can be no doubt that it played a role in the fateful decision by University College Dublin to move out to Belfield. As Arthur Gibney put it, "we are not an urban people and we have no consciousness of urban values". Our antipathy to the city is reflected even in the smallest ways. When the Corporation completed its housing scheme on Rutland Street Upper, off Summerhill, a decision was made to re-name the street in honour of playwright Sean O'Casey. But instead of calling it Sean O'Casey Street, the suburban form of Avenue was adopted. And two years ago, at the end of a round-table discussion on RTE radio's "Live Line" programme, Marian Finucane asked her guests if they had important foreign visitors coming to Dublin, where would be the first place they would take them? Incredibly, city manager Frank Feely replied: "The Dublin Mountains".

But then, almost all of the people who make decisions about Dublin tend to live in the suburbs and the city has become a sort of colony which they drive in to administer, five days a week. Their view of the place is very largely the view of the suburban motorist, and they see nothing wrong with sacrificing its fabric to cater for cars. After all, it could be argued, there is hardly anybody left in the inner city - or, at least, hardly anybody who counts - so it's fair game to transform historic streets into dual-carriageways to serve the majority who now live in suburbs. The inhabitants of the ghetto have more immediate concerns than "the environment" - such as where the next meal is going to come from - and, in any case, they do not have access to anyone in authority even if they wanted to make a protest.

Many of the threats to the city's fabric stem from what one architect called "the Chamber of Commerce view of the city" - the idea that Dublin is essentially a commercial enterprise and, therefore, the central business district must take precedence over everything else. Above all, it has to be "accessible" to car-borne commuters and shoppers alike - even if this means that residential areas along the main routes into town must be destroyed to make way for them. It is surely no coincidence that the most favoured inner city residential enclave, in and around the South Circular Road, is not threatened by road-widening schemes. Nobody with a choice, other than the Corporation's own tenants, is going to live beside a major dual-carriageway.

The attitude of the administration, that the city is essentially disposable if it gets in the way of traffic, is reinforced by an unsympathetic view of architecture which sees old buildings in pathological terms, as if they were decaying bodies. This was put in a nutshell by John Prendergast, the assistant city and county manager who presides over the planning department, when he was asked at a public meeting in the Mansion House in April 1988 why there was so much dilapidation in the inner city. His explanation - which would be greeted with astonishment throughout Europe - was that most of the area's building stock is more than seventy years old and is, therefore, "well past its prime". In other words, buildings - like people - have a fixed life expectancy which cannot be extended and once they reach the end of their useful life, if not demolished for redevelopment, they will eventually fall down, killing some poor unfortunate in the street.

The Corporation's view of old buildings as liabilities rather than assets is reflected in the summons-like notice it sends to people whose properties are being listed for preservation. (Those with houses on the road-widening hit list are told nothing, of course). Yet the idea that new buildings are necessarily better than older ones does not stand up to scrutiny; almost two dozen modern office blocks built in Dublin over the past 20 years have had to be substantially rebuilt because of serious defects - including structural faults - while many Georgian houses remain sound today, even after 200 years. In other European cities, buildings much older than Dublin's are surviving still. Age alone is rarely the real problem, just proper maintenance.

But the Corporation's myopia is coloured by two factors. Firstly, for almost 70 years now, its officials have looked at the inner city as little better than a slum which needs to be cleared and, secondly, the city's architectural heritage has too often been viewed in the context of the dangerous buildings code, with devastating effects on its fabric. The almost foolhardy heroism of individuals taking on the task of restoring decrepit Georgian houses is given no official encouragement; indeed, they are regarded as a band of eccentrics, at best. Senior Corporation officials simply cannot fathom why anyone would even want to restore a decaying 18th century "tenement", still less live in one, when there are such fine modern houses in the suburbs - more often than not, indeed, with mock-Georgian PVC windows and porticoes in the finest fibreglass money can buy. Like the traditional thatched cottages of rural Ireland, the tenements of Georgian Dublin are associated with an era of poverty which they would prefer to forget.

Conservation, like lunch in the film *Wall Street*, is for wimps. It is viewed as a namby-pamby concern, unlike demolition and redevelopment which is so obviously *macho* in character. Nobody in power, in central or local government, has seen the city for what it is - a cultural asset of immense importance. Instead, Ministers regard the centre of Dublin as a convenient quarry for the construction industry and they talk in terms of the number of jobs which will be created by this or that development. They have an almost child-like urge to see cranes on the skyline and bulldozers on the ground, because these are the most potent symbols of "progress", in the tired old 1960s meaning of the word. They forget that the real issue is what the bulldozers and cranes leave behind, to stand on the street for, perhaps, a century or more. After all, nobody knows, or even cares, how many jobs were created 200 years ago when James Gandon built the Custom House. What we do know is that Dublin would be much poorer as a city if such great classical buildings as the Custom House had not been built.

There is also a vogue for the ersatz. Having destroyed the medieval city by driving dual-carriageways through it, the authorities at State and local level are now considering a plan to "reconstruct" old Dublin as a sort of Bunratty-style "theme park" on a derelict site at Bride Street and Golden Lane. And just like the Bunratty Folk Park, this would be little more than an architectural zoo where visitors could see a representative selection of Dublin buildings from the period 1250 to 1685. Ersatz ideas, verging on kitsch, are also embodied in British Land's vast new shopping centre on St. Stephen's Green, which gobbled up a total of 70 mainly Georgian properties in the cause of "comprehensive redevelopment". Meant to evoke the Curvilinear Range of glasshouses in the National Botanic Gardens, it looks instead like a Mississippi riverboat which has somehow been stranded on the edge of the Green - without its paddle-wheels. Even in its dying days, South King Street was full of interest, with a whole range of shops dealing in antiques, books and bric-a-brac. Now its entire south side has been reduced to a row of door-less "shopfronts", topped by a brick facade mimicking the Gaiety Theatre and the most cluttered roofline in the city, full of flues, ducts and vents.

It is doubtful if any Government Minister, or Corporation official, would recognise the description of Dublin penned by architecture critic Dan Cruickshank in the Observer magazine of October 30th, 1988. "Dublin is one of the great European cities", he wrote. "The design and grandeur of its public buildings, the nobility of its domestic architecture and the beauty of its town plan - with its squares, riverside terraces and generous streets - make it a city second to none. It stands alongside Venice, Rome, Amsterdam and Bath as a supreme example of the city as a corporate work of art. And this is still true of Dublin, even after years of heart-destroying demolitions. Sadly, it is doubtful whether it will still be true a decade from now. If plans proposed for the city come to fruition, and if the national and local governments' disregard for the historic fabric of the city continues, then the character of Dublin will be destroyed and Europe will have lost one of its great monuments to urban civilisation''.

Those who argue along these lines - such as Ian Lumley, the energetic and authoritative planning spokesman for An Taisce - are officially regarded as idealists, wildly out of touch with reality. "People like Lumley are trying to push the toothpaste back into the tube, and the degree to which they want things preserved is so absolute that they frighten developers and politicians", Noel Carroll, the Corporation's inimitable public relations officer told the New York Times in February 1989. "The challenge facing us is in getting the balance between allowing the city to adapt and preserving that which is historic and worthy of preservation". However, as the article made clear, "scores of houses and shops have been torn down" and several cherished pubs - "places of joy that serve as Ireland's extension of the family livingroom" - are threatened with demolition to make way for the Corporation's road plans.

To the extent that architectural conservation figures at all in official thinking, it is tied to the limited notion of preserving the great monuments. City manager Frank Feely often marvels at the fact that, of the 19 important buildings depicted in James Malton's prints, 17 of them are still there. (The two casualties to "progress" were the Tholsel, in Christchurch Place, and the Marine School on Sir John Rogerson's Quay). But this should hardly be a source of amazement, even to a man who has been a Corporation official since he left school in 1949. Any city with a degree of civility would preserve its great monuments. What divides the great cities from the mean ones is their attitude towards ordinary buildings - the houses, shops and pubs - and the extent to which they are cherished, or neglected, says much about the priorities of city fathers and citizens alike.

The city manager told *In Dublin* in February 1988 that he regarded himself as a conservationist, citing the money spent on City Hall and the Municipal Gallery as evidence of the Corporation's commitment to architectural conservation. In fact, the Corporation's record in property management is deplorable. The Iveagh Baths, probably the most important *art nouveau* building in Ireland, has been allowed to fall into decay. Thomas Street library was abandoned and its condition was allowed to deteriorate to such a degree that the dangerous buildings section ordered the top floor to be taken down. The Victorian buildings in Castle Street formerly occupied by the Corporation's engineers were left unsecured after the department moved into the Civic Offices and, later, destroyed by arson because security was so inadequate. The Black Church on Mountjoy Place, with its remarkable parabolic vault, built to the designs of John Semple in 1830, is rotting away quitely after almost 25 years in the hands of the Corporation. And despite all of the efforts made by private owners to clean up their buildings for the Millennium - most spectacularly, the ICS Building Society's revelation of the Scots baronial pile at the apex of D'Olier Street and Westmoreland Street - the Central Fire Station in Tara Street with its Florentine campanile remains one of the dirtiest buildings in the centre of Dublin.

Another public body, the City of Dublin Vocational Education Committee, has been guilty of what An Taisce described as "wanton neglect of security and appalling property management" in recent years. And the inevitable consequence of this was the destruction by fire of the former Jacob's biscuit factory in Bishop Street, in May 1987, five years after the VEC had purchased the property for £1.25 million. The previous December, An Taisce wrote to the VEC expressing grave concern about the fact that the buildings - which were earmarked for conversion into a new premises for the College of Commerce - had been left "wide open to entry". But they received no response to queries about what security arrangements, if any, were being provided. Letters from An Taisce to the VEC's chief executive, Liam Arundel, about the fate of two very important Georgian houses in Parnell Square which had been abandoned by the College of Marketing and Design for a rented office block in Mountjoy Square, also went unanswered. And as a direct result of the absence of adequate security, several magnificent 18th century marble fireplaces were stolen from the houses and sold on the London market for substantial sums of money.

The example set by the Government is not much better. True, the restoration of the Custom House is a superlative achievement and the Office of Public Works also deserves credit for the improvements to the Phoenix Park, the landscaping of the Casino at Marino (even if this is somewhat belated) and the fine restoration of the Senate Chamber ceiling in Leinster House. But there is a darker side to the record. Directly opposite the Taoiseach's Department on Upper Merrion Street, where Ministers in successive governments have been pictured arriving for Cabinet meetings, a whole terrace of Georgian houses in State ownership is being allowed to go derelict - despite the fact that a

In a playful mood... the City Manager, Frank Feely, poses for photographers, trying a Viking helmet for size, during the visit of a Danish sail training vessel in September 1987. (Photograph: The Irish Times).

The Third World comes to North King Street... free range chickens and piebald ponies on a derelict site near the Special Criminal Court awaiting the arrival of the Inner Tangent. (Photograph: Pat Langan).

restoration scheme was drawn up in 1986. The old Palm House and Curvilinear Range in the National Botanic Gardens, Glasnevin, masterpieces of Victorian architecture, are literally falling apart. Beggars Bush Barracks lies substantially abandoned, with a massive modern office block plonked in the middle of it. And the one-time Jameson Distillery buildings in Smithfield, including the impressive stone warehouses on Bow Street, present a picture of "horrifically advancing dereliction", as An Taisce put it, after 17 years in State ownership. In June 1989, as a direct consequence of official neglect, a major portion of the Bow Street frontage had to be demolished after vandals set fire to it.

Not every public institution has a deplorable record of building maintenance. Trinity College, which occupies the largest single group of historic buildings in the city, has set an exemplary record for architectural conservation in recent years under the leadership of its Provost, Dr Bill Watts. A scheme to demolish the entire west side of Westland Row - including Oscar Wilde's house - to make way for a series of gable-fronted modern blocks was abandoned, much to the distress of the Corporation's road engineers who had their eye on widening it. Now the early 19th century terrace is to be refurbished, with new buildings erected at the rear, like Scott Tallon Walker's recently completed O'Reilly Institute. Even more spectacular was De Blacam and Meagher's restoration of the mid-18th century Dining Hall, which was nearly destroyed by fire in 1984, and the erection alongside it of a superb galleried atrium, hewn out of the old kitchen block. There are also exciting plans for the Pearse Street frontage, including student accommodation and a theatre dedicated to Samuel Beckett, with completion timed to coincide with Trinity's 400th birthday in 1992.

In a special supplement on Dublin as long ago as 1974, the *Architectural Review* drew particular attention to the plight of the Liffey Quays. "While picturesque decay may have its attractions as the subject for a painting, to allow structures to rot as they are doing along the Liffey quays is disastrous, for these riverside buildings are the essential Dublin", said the *AR*. "Individually unremarkable as works of architecture, collectively they are superb, and form a perfect foil to the special buildings, such as the Four Courts and the Custom House". And it declared that the success of any move to restore Dublin "may be fairly measured by whether or not it brings to the quays a return to prosperity and coherence".

The great cut-stone wall of the former Jameson Distillery warehouses on Bow Street, before the mid-section was demolished after a fire in June 1989. (Photograph: The Irish Times).

Fifteen years later, the Liffey quays are in a worse state than ever. Instead of being restored, many of the buildings which the *AR* found to be dilapidated have since been demolished. In some cases, whole terraces of buildings have been pulled down, to be replaced by blue Corporation hoardings pending redevelopment. Parts of the quays, especially at the western end, are still affected by road plans and one notable casualty waiting for the chop, is the Georgian house on Ushers Island where James Joyce set his most famous short story, *The Dead*. And despite the renewed interest in the riverfront, even as a prospect for residential development, there is no plan indicating what would be acceptable and what would not. The planners simply wait for the developers to move in, reacting to their proposals instead of drawing up a plan themselves. Over it all loom the Corporation's own offices, the two great bunkers on Wood Quay, which were built on the most important Viking site ever excavated in Europe despite an unprecedented outpouring of public protest. The bureaucrats wanted their offices and bloody-mindedly made sure to get them, whatever the people had to say about it.

But if Dubliners expect a more enlightened view from their elected representatives, they would be sadly disappointed. Indeed, out of the City Council's 52 members, not much more than half-a-dozen could be said to have a grasp of the city's problems, in any real sense. The rest are so pre-occupied with looking after the narrowly-defined needs of their own electoral areas - getting windows repaired or back lanes re-paved - that they simply haven't developed a Dublin-wide view. And like the Know Nothings of old, they make no effort to broaden their horizons. In the spring of 1988, for example, when Professor Frank Convery, of UCD, staged a series of seminars on the theme "Revitalising Dublin - What Works?", which went right to the core of the city's problems, only a handful of the councillors i othered to attend. Had it been held in Helsinki, many would have been fighting for tickets.

In 1985, when the present council was ele ted, there was some hope that it would see the city in a new, more positive l ht. The large Fianna Fail group, at the instigation of their party leader, Mr Haughey, took a bus tour of the problem areas with Professor Kevin B. Nowlan, chairman of the Dublin Civic Group and former president of An Taisce. But all councillors go through the same cycle. In the first flush of enthusiasm, they believe that they can change things. Gradually, they begin to realise that the city is, in fact, run by the Corporation officials rather than the elected representatives of the people. They are irritated by this odd arrangement and would like to do something about it, but because of the nature of clientilist politics they depend on the officials to look after their parochial concerns so that they can service their constituents. And in no time at all, they find themselves locked in a symbiotic relationship and any criticism of the Corporation, though it's directed at the officials who really run the show, they come to regard as a criticism of themselves. In short, they are "enlisted" by the bureaucrats.

SAVING THE CITY

Dublin county councillors don't see the city at all, though they meet in a sound-proofed chamber on the ground-floor of an office block in O'Connell Street. To them, the city appears as a formless white blob on their zoning maps, and they simply ignore it, concentrating instead on "Section 4" motions and other devices to facilitate developers who want planning permission for houses or shops on the periphery. In the absence of any metropolitan authority, there is little or no consideration given to the strategic impact of, say, the development of a large-scale suburban housing estate or shopping centre on the rest of Dublin - particularly the inner city. It is almost as if it didn't exist.

At the Dublin Crisis Conference in February 1986, a large attendance representing over 100 community, environmental and other interest groups throughout the city unanimously adopted a resolution which called on the Government and the Dublin local authorities "to recognise and accept that the city is in crisis". However, there is no indication that this was ever taken on board, either by the bureaucrats or the politicians. If anything, especially during the Millennium, the standard line was that Dublin was wonderful, that everything the Corporation did was wonderful, and anyone who suggested otherwise was a "begrudger". Yet if they don't admit that there is a serious problem to be solved, how can they set about solving it?

An extreme example of officialdom's capacity for self-delusion was the reaction of former Lord Mayor Ben Briscoe to the news that Dublin had been ranked 101st among European cities, in a survey by economists from Reading University. (Frankfurt was first and Liverpool last, in 117th place). "I resent Dublin being placed 101st", Mr Briscoe declared. "I have travelled extensively and I would put Dublin in the top 10. I often tell Americans that if they visit Europe without seeing Dublin, it is like visiting India without seeing the Taj Mahal". As Colm Toibin noted in the *Sunday Independent*, the survey had its absurdities - squeaky clean West German cities did really well and there was little recognition for lively places like Lisbon or Barcelona - but Dublin was such a "deeply degraded city" that Mr Briscoe was surely thinking of Calcutta, rather than the Taj Mahal, he said.

The Cheshire Report, as the comparative survey of cities is known, was undertaken in 1988 on behalf of the EC Commission. Based on a range of economic and social indices, it identified Dublin as one of 14 urban areas which had "seriously deteriorated" since 1974, when the last survey was undertaken. It also showed that Dublin is one of only three urban areas within the European Community which has urban problems of both decline and growth, caused by the outward flow of population and employment from the core to new suburban areas on the periphery. It found that these problems were exacerbated by "strong forces of inertia" and recommended that the EC should give priority to assisting cities like Dublin, which it classified as being among the worst 21-35% of urban areas within the Community.

Privately, many officials in central and local government are so mesmerised by the scale of the problem that they seem incapable of taking any effective action. Solutions are being suggested, but from outside the power structure, and there is a broad consensus on what needs to be done which embraces bodies as diverse as Combat Poverty and the Royal Institute of the Architects of Ireland. But though the draft city development plan includes a commitment to "community planning", there is no sign that this is taken seriously by the bureaucracy. Concerned citizens are still treated as cranks, and letters to the Corporation seeking information on its policies often go unanswered, even when they come from An Taisce, a prescribed body under the Planning Acts.

In 1988, the city celebrated its Millennium. Everybody knew that it was a bogus event, since historians had long fixed 841 AD as the year in which Dubhlinn was founded by the Vikings so, to that extent, the "anniversary" came 147 years too late. But the city manager wanted some sort of celebration - and quickly - and he decided to hang his millennium on an event which happened in 988 AD when the Vikings of Dublin submitted to Malachy, the High King of Ireland. The Irish, under Malachy, had laid siege to Dublin, which they had sacked previously on several occasions, and the Vikings were determined that this would not happen again. So they agreed to abase themselves before the High King and give him his Tribute of Gold for one simple reason - *to save the city from destruction.*

Yet one thousand years later, in a bitter historical irony, we were invited to celebrate the anniversary of this event by the very people who are destroying the city from within through their plans to reshape it for cars - at the cost of demolishing literally hundreds of buildings. Indeed, Dublin Corporation's - and the Government's - principal contribution to the city in its millennium year was to transform once-bustling Parnell Street into a major dual-carriageway, with instant trees and cobblelock pavements replacing pubs, shops and guesthouses in terraces of three- and four-storey Georgian buildings. As Deirdre Kelly, of the Living City Group, observed: "Recently, the engineers discovered trees. Maybe, in time, they will also discover that it is buildings which make a streetscape''.

The Millennium was a circus, its high-point the parading of a gigantic inflatable Gulliver through the streets, but at least it put a spotlight on the city, generating a great wave of goodwill which could - and hopefully will - make a real, lasting impact. But though there is an emerging consensus that the plans being pursued by those in authority will only succeed in destroying the city, there is no indication that the Government or the Corporation will take a blind bit of notice; the Millennium did nothing to change their perceptions. They seem doggedly determined to stay on course, making the same ghastly mistakes that other cities made 20 or 30 years ago, and using European Community funds to pay for a lot of it.

Way back in June 1971, in a remarkably prescient analysis of the state of Dublin, the great planning philosopher Lewis Mumford said that it exhibited "the worst qualities of both provincial isolation and metropolitan aggrandisement. It is on the way to becoming a nonentity". The new suburban estates "show hardly a hint of what we have learned about planning, with their long monotonous row housing", he declared. "They do not form real neighbourhoods - they are adjuncts to shopping centres". The core of Dublin he described as "a real city", though suffering "obvious displacement and inner re-building, but little inner city renewal". And he concluded: "The first step in planning today is to stop doing the wrong things! A city can be destroyed by bad highways and building in a few years''.

Five years before Mumford delivered his warning, the equally far- sighted architect, planner and conservationist Uinseann MacEoin gave a similar diagnosis in *Build* magazine: "If the present policy is pursued to its logical conclusion, Dublin will become a Great Dead City with pockets of working class flats in Greek Street, Benburb Street, Dominick Street, Cook Street and Vicar Street, a mere shadow of what it was once", he warned. "There will be less than half the population of fifty years ago living in the central area (between the two circular roads) while outside and beyond it in the concreted wilderness of Ballyfermot, Artane, West Finglas and Coolock, Cappagh and Clonee, there will be anything up to three quarters of a million people". Those lines were written in August 1966, over 23 years ago, so nobody in authority can say that they weren't told.

Before and after the deluge... a photograph of Parnell Street taken in 1975, before the Corporation got its hands on it (above) and, below, a view of the same section of the street in May, 1989, after the dual-carriageway had been completed. The lamp post in each photograph is the same. (Photographs: Irish Architectural Archive and Pat Langan).

The lost city...a view of Cornmarket in 1918 (above) and (below) the same view 70 years later. The tall limestone building in the centre of each picture is the same building. (Photographs: Colin Scudds).

Groundscraper...an aerial view of the St. Stephen's Green Shopping Centre, just before it opened in late-1988. The Green Cinema (left) has since been demolished and the site is currently used as a surface car park - illegally, at the time of writing. (Photograph issued by the developers, British Land).

2

A Question of Transport

The transport issue is critical, since the whole future of the city is bound up with it - whether Dublin develops into a mini-Los Angeles, by continuing to give primacy to the private car, or follows the more civilised model of European cities by developing a fast, efficient public transport system. The still dominant view, accepted at the highest levels of Dublin Corporation and the Department of the Environment, is that catering for cars is the natural order of things and the way to solve the problem of congestion is to build more roads. However, as Marshall McLuhan once said in a letter to the Premier of Ontario, opposing plans for a highway through Toronto, "Mere concern with efficient traffic flow is a cloacal obsession that sends the city down the drain". And in most other European capitals, it is now widely recognised that traffic expands to fill the road space available, causing more congestion and pollution in the long-term. Indeed, the only major European city, apart from Dublin, that's still bulldozing its buildings to cater for cars is the one which seems closest to the Third World - Istanbul.

In a best-selling book, *The Costs of Economic Growth*, Professor E.J. Mishan of the London School of Economics described traffic congestion in cities as "the most notorious by-product of industrialization the world has ever known". And he went on: "One consequence is that the pleasures of strolling along the streets of a city are more of a memory than a current past-time. Lorries, motorcycles and taxis belching fumes, filth and stench, snarling engines and unabating visual disturbance have compounded to make movement through a city an ordeal for the pedestrian at the same time as the mutual strangulation of the traffic makes it a purgatory for motorists. The formula of mend -and-make-do followed by successive transport ministers (in Britain) is culminating in a maze of one-way streets, peppered with parking meters, with massive signs, detours and weirdly-shaped junctions and circuses across which traffic pours from several directions, while penned-in pedestrians jostle each other along narrow pavements. Towns and cities have been rapidly transmogrified into roaring workshops, the authorities watching anxiously as the traffic builds up with no policy other than that of spreading the rash of parking meters to discourage the traffic on the one hand and, on the other, to accommodate it by road-widening, tunnelling, bridging and patching up here and there; perverting every principle of amenity a city can offer in the attempt to force through it the growing traffic. This 'policy' - apparently justified by reckoning as social benefits any increase in the volume of traffic and any increase in its average speed - would, if it were pursued more ruthlessly, result inevitably in a Los Angeles-type solution in which the greater part of the metropolis is converted to road space; in effect a city buried under roads and freeways''.

For too long in Dublin, the car has been king, and the Corporation, in its single-minded effort to cater for car-borne commuters, has destroyed much of the older part of the city with roads and plans for roads. High Street, once the main street of the medieval city, has been turned into a transit zone for cars, and the same fate has befallen or still awaits many other streets in the city. Not only is the pattern of the old streets destroyed, but the buildings disappear as well, rarely to be replaced, and life for the remaining inhabitants of the inner city is made more intolerable. As Nuala O Faolain wrote in *The Irish Times:* "Everywhere the road engineers have had their way is empty and dead; everywhere they have spared teems with life". And, addressing herself to the city councillors, she asked: "Can't they see that Meath Street, for example, is a whole interesting world, and that Bridgefoot Street, for example, is a desert?"

Take the case of Parnell Street. It is hard to believe, looking at it now, that this street was once a lively part of the city centre, lined with terraces of three- and four-storey buildings. As Nuala O Faolain noted in her article, these buildings contained "seven pubs, six butchers, three bookies, two shoe repairers, two chemists, a watchmaker, a cafe, a guesthouse, four small factories and 26 other shops". All of this has now been swept away, to be replaced by the back entrance of the ILAC shopping centre, a multi-storey car park and a mixture of dwarf walls, "amenity trees", slatted timber fences, brick-paved footpaths and traditional-style lamp standards. These latter features are apparently regarded by the road engineers as a suitable "environmental treatment" for the edge of the new dual-carriageway, but in no sense could they be seen as an adequate replacement for all the buildings - and the businesses - which have been obliterated. Indeed, combined with the large surface car park on the north side of the street, the Corporation's "environmental treatment" merely serves to underline the dramatic loss of any sense of a city in this area.

And what of the cost? Trying to quantify this, in purely financial terms, is an immensely difficult task because of a basic unwillingness to make the figures available. It is made even more problematic because the road plans are all judged in isolation, piece by piece, without any assessment of what the final bill will be or whether, indeed, it is worth paying at all. According to a study by Dr P.J. Drudy, lecturer in economics at Trinity College, the Parnell Street scheme works out at up to £15.7 million per mile (in 1987 prices) - and figures provided to the City Council in March 1989 indicated that it could even be higher, at £17 million per mile. This would include the cost of property acquisition and demolition - rarely given by the engineers in their published estimates - as well as the bare cost of building the road, which usually accounts for only a fraction of the total. However, the estimate does not include interest charges on borrowed money - which are always included "above the line" for public transport investments - nor does it include the substantial cost, ultimately borne by the community, of reinstating a line of new buildings alongside the completed dual-carriageways.

Given the devastation wrought so expensively in Parnell Street and the evidence of other "completed" road schemes where, as likely as not, the new street frontages are lined with derelict sites and advertising hoardings, it is little wonder that more and more Dubliners are opposed to what the road engineers are planning for the city. And one of the main reasons why there is so much concern about the road plans is that people can see that roads and streets determine the shape of the city, for good or ill; it is around them that the city is built. This was well understood by the Wide Streets Commissioners in the late 18th century when they gave Dublin such fine thoroughfares as D'Olier Street, Westmoreland Street and O'Connell Street. The Commissioners had a vision of the city and it was through their efforts that Dublin gained what grandeur it still has today. For the road engineers to cite the achievements of the Wide Streets Commissioners as a model for what the Corporation has in mind today is a total distortion, like their oft-repeated claim that the completed dual-carriageways will resemble Lower Baggot Street, with its cherry trees in blossom.

What makes Baggot Street so attractive is the fact that it is largely lined with four-storey-over-basement Georgian houses, so there is a proportional relationship between the width of the street and the height of the buildings. The engineers also neglect to note that the Department of the Environment - which provides 100 per cent of the funding required for road "improvements" in the city - makes no provision for the reinstatement of streetscapes, after the roads are put through. Thus, as Alderman Carmencita Hederman has pointed out, Cuffe Street was still left with "unsightly gables, blocked-up windows and fireplaces, corrugated iron and partly demolished walls" fifteen years after it was turned into a major dual-carriageway. The city manager, Frank Feely, responded by saying merely that it was "regrettable that there should be such a time lapse between acquisition and development".

Yet if the Corporation could not get anyone to build an "imposing" building right at the corner of St Stephen's Green, what chance is there that this will happen in North King Street, for example? Indeed, senior planners concede that they are likely to get little more than "warehouse uses" on the route of the Inner Tangent - functional gable-fronted sheds replacing still decent Georgian or Victorian buildings. This is on the cards for the simple reason that most of the road plans affect areas which are "soft" targets - in other words, they are more dilapidated and, therefore, easier to acquire than "hard" areas, like Ballsbridge. What this also means is that rental levels are low, so there is little prospect of developers moving in to build shops, office blocks or apartment buildings along the route of the Inner Tangent. In any case, who would want to work - or live - on the edge of this traffic machine? Far from the "tree-lined avenues" of the engineers' imagination, it would be "a formidable road, forbidding to pedestrians", according to the deputy chief planning officer, Pat McDonnell. It would also be noisy, dirty and polluted by traffic fumes, he said candidly in 1987, and "won't be like a Continental boulevard".

But whatever about the damage done to the city by their plans, the road engineers in the Corporation and the Department of the Environment are sustained by a powerful lobby which includes the Confederation of Irish Industry (CII), the Dublin Chamber of Commerce, the Construction Industry Federation and the various civil engineering companies with a direct interest

Delaney's public house in North King Street which could be reprieved if the City Council decides to drop the "outer leg" of the Inner Tangent road scheme. (Photograph by Peter Thursfield).

in road construction. The CII Newsletter, in May 1987, did not even attempt to disguise where it stood by uttering the usual platitudes about the importance of having a "balanced transportation policy". It said that private transport accounts for 95 per cent of total household spending on transport, that traffic is "the life blood of modern commerce", that cars are "here to stay" and, since their utility value is "greatly diminished by an inadequate road network", public investment was required to bring the roads up to an acceptable standard. Echoing the view of assistant city manager Sean Haughey, the CII newsletter declared that "omelettes cannot be made without breaking eggs".

The breaking of those eggs has been pursued with single-minded determination by the roads and traffic department, which was headed by Mr Haughey, a brother of the Taoiseach, until he retired in 1989 after 48 years service with the Corporation. Most notorious, undoubtedly, is the case of the Good Times Bar, at the corner of Lower Kevin Street, which was demolished during the General Election campaign in February 1987 when many councillors had more pressing things on their minds. Indeed, so anxious were the officials to get rid of this key building, which stood in the way of the Inner Tangent road scheme, that demolition work started just one week after the Corporation had paid £250,000 for the premises. Later, when councillors complained about what had happened to this fine Victorian public house, the roads department cited "professional advice that the lack of a proper left turning facility from Kevin Street Lower to Redmonds Hill has resulted in traffic that would have made the turn taking the alternative 'rat-run' through Bishop Street ..... Hence the advantage of implementing the interim scheme". But this justification was specious because it is a fact that the volume of traffic using the new "filter lane" is very low indeed, and Bishop Street - which is still the shortest route - remains as plagued by "rat-running" as ever. The real value to the officials of getting the Good Times Bar out of the way became apparent at a City Council committee meeting six months after the demolition, when one of them told the councillors that there was little left in Lower Kevin Street which would be worth preserving. There was some irony in the fact that the planners have since recommended listing the Parliament Inn, a handsome four-storey pub building in Parliament Street, which looks almost exactly like the Good Times Bar.

Though blatant, the case of the Good Times Bar is far from unique - judging by the example of Ellis Quay, which had been on the Corporation's hit list for many years. At a general purposes committee meeting in July 1987, one of a series called to "consider" the road plans, councillors asked whether there were any buildings left there. They were told by Maurice McMonagle, senior roads engineer, that the last two survivors were "gone" or "probably gone", because "we (the Corporation) own them". This was challenged by Councillor Tony Gregory TD, who said he was sure they were still there. He then requested that, since the councillors were to be taken on a bus tour of the areas affected by the road plans, the two late-Victorian buildings - formerly a chemist's and a jeweller's - should not be demolished, at least until members of the committee had got a chance to see them.

An hour or so later, this writer cycled up to Ellis Quay to find a Corporation demolition crew scrambling over the roofs of the two buildings, stripping them of slates. Later, I discovered that the officials had been so anxious to gain possession of one of these buildings that they had sought to get the keys at 11 am, five hours ahead of the time specified in the contract of sale. Was the purpose of this indecent haste to ensure that, by the time the Ellis Quay road-widening plan was presented to the councillors, the surviving buildings would indeed be "gone" and, as in the case of the Good Times Bar, there would be nothing left to argue about? One thing is certain - the two buildings had been reduced to a heap of rubble when the councillors passed by on their bus tour. But Sean Haughey was able to cite a committee decision, in the dim and distant past, approving plans for a Corporation housing scheme on Ellis Quay which clearly implied that the existing buildings would be demolished.

There is a major question mark over how the Corporation managed to gain such a foothold in and around Ellis Quay. The compulsory purchase order (CPO) for the area was made under the Housing Act, ostensibly for the purpose of building houses there, though the main objective all along was road-widening. Indeed, by the time a "public inquiry" into the CPO was held, in June 1985, the Corporation owned all but two of the properties involved. However, when a question was raised at the two-hour "inquiry" about the road plan for Ellis Quay, which long pre-dated any intention to build housing there, it was ruled out of order on the grounds that it was "not relevant" to the CPO. Just two years later, the Corporation put the entire site on the market, for redevelopment by the private sector under the urban renewal tax incentives, and the scheme of 108 private flats planned for the site was forced to take account of the road -widening proposal.

So far, the only Corporation road plan which has been subjected to a searching public examination is the controversial scheme to drive a dual-carriageway through Patrick Street, New Street and Lower Clanbrassil Street. But even here, the road planners eventually got their way (more or less) in spite of widespread public opposition and a strong appeal to the city council "to take the initiative to halt the destruction of Dublin" from 15 organisations, ranging from the Association of Combined Residents Associations to the Royal Institute of the Architects of Ireland.

The Corporation had already suffered a major setback in June 1986 when both the Fianna Fail leader, Mr Haughey, and the then Taoiseach, Dr FitzGerald, intervened to call for the plan to be re-examined - even though it had already been approved, without amendment, by the then Minister for the Environment, John Boland. But they lost no time in trying to make up for this apparent reversal. As a first step towards reinstating the dual-carriageway scheme, senior Corporation officials encouraged the formation of a pro-road group in the area, the Clanbrassil Street Residents and Traders Association, by telling those involved - mainly people with property blighted for years by the CPO - that there was little or no prospect of them getting their compensation unless the road plan was approved.

The Corporation's strategy - enthusiastically supported by Fianna Fail councillor and later Lord Mayor Ben Briscoe TD, who was working very closely with the officials - was to put forward the traders association as an authentic voice representing the people of the area. But this soon fell apart with the emergence of an articulate locally-based group called RESCUE (an acronym for Residents Eager to Save Clanbrassil Street's Urban Environment), which launched a vigorous campaign against the Corporation's dual-carriageway scheme, arguing instead that any widening should be limited to a maximum of 60 feet - which also happened to be the widest point on the existing street. But in November 1986, six months after the City Council put the New Street/ Clanbrassil Street road plan on ice, the roads department sought to pre-empt such a solution by gutting the pair of Victorian red-brick buildings which were standing at that wide point. Again, a specious justification was offered - viz, that some of the stair treads inside were rotten and, if anyone broke into the vacant buildings and fell down the stairs, the Corporation might be held responsible. When the demolition was halted, at the insistence of city councillors, one of their number - Joe Burke (FF), who represents the Clontarf area - expressed concern that Corporation workers who

The Good Times Bar at the corner of Kevin Street and Redmond's Hill before it was acquired by the Corporation for £250,000 in early 1987 and demolished one week later and (below) the same corner as it is today. (Photographs: The Irish Times and Pat Langan).

The former distillery offices of Watkins, Jameson and Pim, on Ardee Street, occupied during the 1916 Rising by Eamonn Ceannt's volunteers, which stand right in the way of the Cork Street/Coombe by-pass road scheme. (Photograph: The Irish Times).

The White House Bar in New Street, blocked up to await demolition for the Corporation's dual-carriageway scheme affecting Patrick Street, New Street and Clanbrassil Street. (Photograph: Pat Langan).

The demolition of Patrick Street in November 1988, showing Joe McDonald's public house in the foreground, just before it was pulled down. (Photograph: The Irish Times).

The Bunch of Grapes pub in Clanbrassil Street, which closed its doors on Ash Wednesday, 1989, blocked up by the Corporation as a prelude to its demolition. (Photograph: Pat Langan).

had been engaged in demolishing buildings in the city might have to be laid off because they had nothing to do.

However, the public campaign against the Corporation's road plan, culminating in a march from Clanbrassil Street to City Hall, did result in at least a partial victory. At a sensational meeting of the City Council in November 1987, with chanting protesters massed outside - Students Against the Destruction of Dublin most prominent among them - the councillors decided by 25 votes to 24 to reject the Corporation's scheme. It was a fluke result. Fianna Fail councillors, who were just short of a majority, could always be counted on to support the road plans, on a whipped party vote, but one of them - the late Ned Brennan - had broken his leg that morning and was unable to attend the meeting while another, local alderman Mary Mooney, openly defied the whip to vote against this particular plan. The Lord Mayor, Carmencita Hederman, later brought together the local councillors and the somewhat shell-shocked officials in an effort to reach an agreed solution, based on a four-lane single carriageway with a maximum width of 68 feet, but the principal officer in the roads department, Paddy Meehan, remained stubbornly adamant that it had to be a dual-carriageway - the very thing local people and their supporters didn't want. He was retiring in a matter of weeks and he wanted to leave the Corporation on a high note, with a victory under his belt.

At a meeting of the City Council's general purposes committee in mid-December, the officials unveiled their own "compromise" proposals. Sean Haughey, assistant city manager in charge of the roads department, sounded quite conciliatory when he explained to the councillors that the officials had looked again at their plans and, though they were still insisting on the road being a dual-carriageway, the overall width would be reduced to 72 feet - instead of the 88 feet originally intended. The Lord Mayor and the councillors representing the Liberties area spoke out strongly against it, however, arguing that the provision of a central median - what transforms an ordinary road into a dual-carriageway - would only encourage speeding. But the officials, and the councillors who supported them, insisted that it was an essential safety feature, providing a "refuge" for pedestrians crossing the road. (The real reason for the central median, however, is that this road is planned as part of a much larger dual-carriageway system, stretching back through Harold's Cross, Kimmage and beyond. But this plan was not presented to the councillors at any stage during the their deliberations).

SAVING THE CITY

The committee meeting went on for two hours and, in the end, the scheme put forward by the officials was adopted by 10 votes to nine. On both sides of the argument, councillors assumed that the compromise width of 72 feet, offered by Mr Haughey, would apply to the whole length of the road, from Christchurch Place almost as far as Leonard's Corner. After all, the agenda for the meeting contained only one item and it read as follows: "Patrick Street/Clanbrassil Street - Development and Road Improvement Scheme". What's more, Councillor Tom Farrell (FG) had sought and received an assurance at a City Council meeting five days earlier that the revised plan for Patrick Street would be available at the general purposes committee meeting on December llth. It was, indeed, "available", but most councillors didn't see it and, at no stage, did the officials tell them where they could find it. Unlike the map showing New Street and Clanbrassil Street, which was pinned up on a board for all to see, the plan for Patrick Street was almost invisible. One of the officials simply sat there with a drawing of it in front of him, and when a councillor who had twigged that it was, in fact, a map of Patrick Steet asked him what the width of the road would be, this official said he couldn't say because he hadn't brought along a ruler to measure it.

The truth, which only emerged at a stormy City Council meeting in January 1988, was that the proposed width of the dual-carriageway on Patrick Street had not been reduced to 72 feet. It remained the same as it always was, at 88 feet, and there was no provision for wider footpaths - as in the revised plans for New Street and Clanbrassil Street - where trees could be planted to screen flats or houses from the noise and fumes of heavy traffic. The sole concession - as agreed in June 1987 at a meeting called by the Taoiseach, Mr Haughey, in his Kinsealy residence - related to the treatment of St Patrick's Cathedral. There, at the insistence of Dean Victor Griffin, the road is to be moved as far away as possible from the west front of the cathedral and, instead of being a dual-carriageway with a solid central median, it is to be divided by a "ghost median" of hatched white lines. But this applies only to the short stretch of road in front of the cathedral. The rest of Patrick Street, where large numbers of people live in the Iveagh Trust flats, will be turned into a major dual-carriageway, almost 90 feet wide. Even Nicholas Street, coming up to Christchurch Place, which could reasonably be regarded as wide enough, is to be widened still further to cater for greater volumes of traffic.

Sean Haughey had an explanation for the radically different perceptions of councillors and officials as to what, precisely, they were supposed to be discussing. He said that there had been "considerable discussion" at the City Council in July 1987 after the members were informed of the meeting in Kinsealy, at which agreement was reached with Dean Griffin on widths for the broad pavement in front of the cathedral. However, according to this reporter's notes, much of the council's discussion was about the propriety, or otherwise, of such matters being arranged at the Taoiseach's home and there was no debate on the revised proposals for Patrick Street. In fact, these proposals were never debated at all, either at City Council or committee level. And by concentrating their attention on Clanbrassil Street, the councillors gave an impression to Mr Haughey and his officials that they were satisfied with the scheme. However, when the council voted by 25 to 24 not to approve the "Patrick Street/ Clanbrassil Street Development and Road Improvement Scheme", they were throwing out the lot and were entitled to assume that it was a case of "back to the drawing boards".

On January 11th, 1988, just eleven days after the beginning of Dublin's Millennium celebrations, the City Council voted for the revised dual-carriageway scheme for Patrick Street, New Street and Lower Clanbrassil Street. Fianna Fail was joined in the vote by Alderman Mary Mooney, who has since regained the party whip, Labour's Michael O'Halloran, Tim Killeen of the Progressive Democrats and by the Fine Gael group, who defended their U-turn on the basis that they couldn't be seen to be opposing everything. Months later, on Remembrance Sunday, while people were attending services in St Patrick's Cathedral, the Corporation had its bulldozers out pulling down what was left of the west side of Patrick Street. More buildings were demolished in Clanbrassil Street and on February 8th 1989 - Ash Wednesday - the Bunch of Grapes pub closed down, its owners departing with a reported £212,000 in compensation. A week or so later, a team of Corporation workers blocked up the doors and windows in preparation for the inevitable arrival of the demolition squad.

In a real sense, *In Dublin* had a point in describing the Patrick Street/ Clanbrassil Street scheme as "The Haughey Family Motorway". It was pushed through by Sean Haughey, the man in charge of the Corporation's roads and traffic department. It was supported in the cause of "progress" by his nephew, Alderman Sean Haughey, who was elected Lord Mayor in July 1989. And there can be little doubt that the Corporation officials were relying on the ever-reliable Fianna Fail whip to get it through the City Council; that, more than anything else, would explain the refusal of Paddy Meehan to compromise over the width, in discussions with the then Lord Mayor, Carmencita Hederman, and other concerned councillors. There can be no doubt either that the Taoiseach, Mr Haughey, could have made good on his earlier promise by instructing the Fianna Fail councillors - as he had done before, in June 1986 - not to support the plan being pursued by the officials, including his own brother Sean. With an imperious wave of his hand, the Taoiseach might have spared the people of the Liberties from the threat posed by the dual-carriage-way, and the compliant Fianna Fail councillors - many of whom have no serious convictions either way - would have done his bidding. But the extent of Mr Haughey's intervention was limited to protecting the fabric of St Patrick's Cathedral in response to representations from "my friend the Dean". He seemed to forget that Dean Victor Griffin himself is very much a part of the Liberties community and, indeed, something of a local hero - especially on the roads issue.

The road engineers lay heavy stress on the fact that their plans date back years, even decades, and that they are a distillation of numerous studies carried out by eminent "experts" - mainly in the 1960s. But just because they have a long pedigree is no reason in itself why they should be supported. *The plans may simply be the wrong plans.* After all, it was a decision by the City Council in 1955 that led to the building of the Civic Offices at Wood Quay. Almost 35 years later, seeing the "bunkers" as they are built, can anyone in Dublin say that it was the right decision, the one that should have been pursued - as it was - through hell or high water? And though CIE's plans for a transportation centre in the Temple Bar area may have seemed reasonable, even desirable, in 1975 (when they were originally mooted), they do not seem so attractive today. Times change, though it takes courage to recognise mistakes and change plans.

It is an undeniable fact that there is no public consensus in favour of the roads strategy which the Corporation is now pursuing - with the full backing of the Government, it must be said. Even leaving aside their devastating effect on the fabric of the city, the Corporation's plans simply won't work because they are based on the 1960s notion that it is possible to "solve" an urban traffic problem by throwing roads at it. Experience abroad, backed up by recent research (notably by Dr Martin Mogridge, a transport specialist at University College London) has shown that the more road space is provided in a city, the more it will fill up with cars - particularly commuter cars - and that the only effective way of easing traffic congestion is to provide a rail- based public transport alternative so that commuters will leave their cars at home. Cities which have tried to do otherwise, by providing bigger and wider roads, now recognise that they made a mistake. Why does Dublin Corporation choose to ignore this fact?

The problem, of course, is that the Corporation is the roads authority for the city and it sees everything from that narrow perspective. Public transport is CIE's responsibility while the Gardai are in charge of traffic and, since the ill-advised abolition of the Dublin Transport Authority, there is no overall body to draw these different "empires" together. Thus, the Corporation employs road engineers and - as its public relations officer Noel Carroll, said some years ago - "you can't blame them for designing roads". Their job is to put forward road plans; otherwise, they would have very little to do - though, for the sake of the city, they would be better employed in *managing* the traffic rather than *catering* for it.

The Government-appointed consultants who carried out a major study of Dublin in the context of Ireland's application for EC Structural Funds refer to this confusion of responsibilities in their report, saying that it had left the city with a conflicting plethora of studies and proposals, most of them dating from the late 1960s or early 1970s. "One cannot escape the conclusion that transportation studies of the period giving rise to this situation were over-concerned with advocacy of particular sectoral objectives at the expense of real analysis of transportation issues and options. Naturally, having a set of proposals which was never capable of being financed resulted in a state of semi-paralysis in planning terms. In addition, where many of the proposals were looked at in more detail, they were found to be inadequate from both an environmental and operational point of view. Given the uncertainty arising from these planning deficiencies and stern local opposition to several key road proposals on environmental grounds, the ambitious set of proposals disintegrated in parts or was substantially changed by attrition. This resulted in a state of transportation planning chaos from which there has never been a complete recovery".

At first sight, Dublin Corporation's draft city development plan seems very reasonable on the whole question of transport. It says that the use of private cars for commuting "results in major congestion on radial routes" (i.e. the main roads leading into the city centre), and this results in "pressure for road improvements and the provision of further car parking". It refers to the current imbalance in the "modal split", with 52 per cent of commuters travelling into town by car and only 34 per cent using public transport, and says the Corporation's policy is that buses and trains "will be the principal means of accommodating the greater share of peak commuter traffic". The draft also talks a lot about achieving a "balanced transportation system", by supporting bus priority measures, facilitating an underground rail link between Heuston and Connolly stations, improving the road circulation system "consistent with environmental amenity", developing pedestrian streets in the city centre, curtailing all-day commuter car parking and providing more facilities for cyclists. And it notes the establishment (by the former Coalition Government) of the Dublin Transport Authority (DTA) with a mandate "to ensure as far as possible the proper and efficient planning and operation of road and rail transport in the Dublin area".

However, these laudable objectives have been well and truly undermined by Government decisions on the transport front. Firstly, the DTA was abolished, allegedly as part of the drive to cut back on public expenditure, so there is now no body charged with promoting public transport in Dublin. And secondly, the Government announced in October 1987 that "no further consideration" would be given to CIE's plans for the extension of DART-type rail services to Tallaght, Clondalkin, Ballyfermot and other suburban areas, the underground link between Heuston and Connolly or the proposed transportation centre in the Temple Bar area. And since this decision was announced, the silence of the former Minister for Tourism and Transport, John Wilson, on transport issues in Dublin has been deafening; it is as if the whole issue no longer counts politically. Thus, the key elements which gave some credibility to the Corporation's "balanced transportation policy" have been removed and, indeed, its own senior planners must go back to the drawing board. They can hardly avoid doing so because, as things stand, all they have been left with are the road plans put forward by their engineering colleagues - and in no sense can these alone be said to constitute a "balanced transportation policy". Indeed, rather than rectify the present serious imbalance between the use of public and private transport, the road plans will simply aggravate the situation.

The central problem on the transport front in Dublin is that far too many commuters travel into town by car, causing traffic congestion on the radial routes and using up valuable space in the city centre for parking. Back in the mid-1960s, when car ownership was less pervasive and there were hardly any high-capacity roads, over half of the city's commuters travelled by public transport. However, according to the most recent "census" of morning peak-time traffic (taken in November 1988), public transport's share has fallen to just over one-third while private cars account for almost 53 per cent. But when a fast, efficient and reliable public transport system is provided, it can be seen to contribute significantly to the relief of traffic congestion. For example, in the limited catchment area served by the DART suburban railway line, electrified in 1984, the "modal split" is radically different to what it is for the city as a whole, with 53 per cent of commuters using public transport and only 39 per cent still travelling by car.

The draft city plan claims that the proposed road schemes are needed "to facilitate movement of goods and people throughout the entire day rather than facilitating commuter traffic flows at peak times" and they include "relief and by-pass routes which seek to protect the city centre core, residential areas and historic areas from the effects of road traffic". Again, this sounds eminently reasonable, but it does not correspond with the reality on the ground. The truth is that wider roads do facilitate peak-time traffic, first and foremost. One need only cite the Corporation's own figures for Dolphin's Barn bridge which show that, in the first six months since it was doubled in width, morning peak-time traffic went up by 17 per cent. And in relation to protecting the city centre core, residential and historic areas, all the evidence shows that the road-widening schemes already implemented have had a devastating effect.

Even the theory behind the Inner Tangent is faulty. The justification advanced for the route is that it will divert through-traffic around the central business district (CBD), allowing for the creation of traffic-free "environmental cells" within this area. However, much of the Tangent route must be regarded not as a traffic distributor but as extensions of arterial roads leading into the city centre. For example, Patrick Street is clearly part of an arterial route leading from the southside suburbs to the city centre, via Clanbrassil Street and New Street, and there is nothing to prevent traffic on this route turning right at Christchurch Place into Lord Edward Street and Dame Street rather than left into High Street, which forms the next stretch of the Tangent. Similarly, traffic coming into the city centre from the north-east, via Summerhill and Parnell Street, could just as easily turn into Marlborough Street or O'Connell Street as stay on the Tangent as it heads towards North King Street.

SAVING THE CITY

The Inner Tangent cannot be seen as a thing in itself, independent of all the other road schemes, because the engineers are also increasing the capacity of most of the arterial roads leading into the city centre. These include, for example, the proposed new Navan Road and the Chapelizod by-pass as well as the Stillorgan Road, which has been completed almost to motorway standard, and such schemes as the widening of New Street and Clanbrassil Street, with its linked dual-carriageway system stretching back through Harold's Cross to the south-western suburbs. Thus, on the basis that traffic expands to fill the space allotted to it, what the Tangent route would do is to distribute even larger volumes of cars around the city centre.

The EC study consultants - a consortium consisting of economists Davy Kelleher and McCarthy (DKM), town planners Reid McHugh and Partners and accountants Stokes Kennedy Crowley (SKC) - were in two minds about the Tangent. They accepted that it would serve an "essential function" in creating environmental cells in the CBD - but recommend the completion only of its "inner loop", which snakes through Cuffe Street, Kevin Street, Patrick Street, High Street, Bride Street, Church Street, North King Street and Parnell Street, west of O'Connell Street. They justified this by saying that the demolition of buildings along this route, as well as the road works already finished, "is probably beyond beyond a point where anything useful could be gained in an environmental sense by not completing the remaining sections".

It is doubtful, however, if the consultants would even have recommended completing the "inner loop" if the City Council, by quite a small margin, had not adopted the Tangent road plan in 1980. This fateful decision paved the way for Parnell Street to be destroyed, along with Patrick Street, Lower Bridge Street and a large part of North King Street, where today ponies, pigs and free-range hens have the run of a fenced-off derelict site just around the corner from the Special Criminal Court. One of the councillors who voted in favour of the Inner Tangent scheme in 1980 was Ben Briscoe, even though - as he admitted to *In Dublin* magazine at the time - he had not made "a specific study" of this road plan, the very centrepiece of the Corporation's strategy. "We must go ahead and do something or we won't be able to move in five years time", he said. "Bad decisions are better than no decisions". (A full list of the City Council roll-call, both for and against the Tangent, is included in Appendix 1).

The consultants make it clear that their recommendation "is conditional on a number of things being done. Firstly, any further work in completing the inner loop of the Inner Tangent route should be preceded by an environmental impact study. Secondly, environmental improvement and redevelopment of buildings along sections of the route which is already constructed should be a priority. Thirdly, plans for the construction of the remaining sections of the route should have an associated programme for environmental treatment, including restoration and redevelopment of properties along the route. Finally, the design of the section remaining to be constructed at North King Street / Bolton Street to Parnell Street should be reconsidered in terms of scale and its impact on the area". The report goes on: "The outer loop and spur roads to it, located mostly to the west of Church Street, are a different matter. They would involve a considerable amount of property demolition and environmental problems which would be very difficult to design around. The strategic arguments for these routes, given a motorway ring to the West and particularly a Port Access Route, are on the evidence available not compelling. The consultants consider that only in very exceptional circumstances, and when justified by a transportation study, should further inner city road-widening proposals be considered. It is recognised, however, that the same proposals in the Clanbrassil Street area are connected to a proposal for a Tallaght busway which may, on examination, provide justification for it". (Ironically, during the course of the long controversy over Clanbrassil Street, this aspect of the Corporation's road plan was never put forward by the officials as a justification for what they were doing).

If the consultants' recommendations were to be accepted, it would spare a whole range of streets from destruction including Pimlico and Thomas Court, Ushers Island, Queen Street and the entire stretch of North King Street to the west of Church Street - incidentally, preserving the setting of Smithfield in the process. It would also mean the end of a particularly fanciful engineering scheme for a tunnel under Church Street to serve motorists who didn't need to turn left or right off the dual-carriageway on North King Street. However, in their "planning blight" justification for completing the Tangent's inner loop, the consultants seem to have given insufficient weight to the fact that at least eight early to mid-Georgian houses on Capel Street are standing in the way; only this would account for their statement that "the main impact of this route on buildings has already happened and, as a consequence, the issue now is not to bring back the past but to finish the route to an acceptable standard''. The eight Capel Street houses, some with interesting interiors, which are threat-

The Blue Lion pub in Parnell Street, mentioned in Ulysses, which is among the four pubs at the eastern end of Parnell Street facing demolition to make way for the Inner Tangent. (Photograph: The Irish Times).

Belleview Buildings in Thomas Court, a fine mansion block of flats, which has long been threatened by the Inner Tangent. (Photograph:The Irish Times).

The 17th century gate piers of Kevin Street Garda Station - formerly the Palace of St. Sepulchre - which are to be demolished to widen the street by 12 feet. (Photograph: The Irish Times).

ened by the scheme, bear eloquent testimony to the fact that still more destruction of the city's historic core would be required to extend the horror of Parnell Street into North King Street, via what once was Ryder's Row.

The biggest "con" of all is the Eastern By-Pass. This is the motorway which would run from Whitehall, on the northside, to Merrion Gates on the south side, crossing Griffith Avenue and Sandymount Strand en route. It is presented as an effort to cater for heavy goods traffic to and from Dublin Port, but even senior officials of the Port and Docks Board would concede (privately) that it is not designed primarily for this purpose. It is also based on the now discredited predictions of the 1971 Dublin Transportation Study (DTS), which forecast that there would be a total of 500,000 vehicles in the eastern region by 1991; two years away from that target date, we have just about reached half that figure. But whatever about forecasts, the inescapable truth is that the Eastern By-Pass will cater primarily for car commuters, especially from the south-eastern suburbs, providing them with an even faster route into the city centre. And it's not as though they need it. As Labour MEP Barry Desmond points out, the area within a mile of the seafront in Blackrock has already seen the most concentrated investment in transport infrastructure anywhere in the country over the past 20 years, and this is not unrelated to the fact that it lies in the area where most of our decision-makers happen to live. To the west is the Stillorgan Road, which on any weekday morning resembles the Hollywood Freeway, with an endless flood of cars streaming towards the city centre. Then, there's the Blackrock By-Pass, linked to Rock Road and Merrion Road, which provides another high-capacity route into town. And finally, right on the edge of Dublin Bay, there is the DART commuter railway line.

But now, under the guise of providing a "port access route", the road planners in the Department of the Environment and the Dublin local authorities are pushing ahead with plans to install yet another major element of transport infrastructure in the same catchment area. We have already seen a glimpse of what lies in store with the controversial decision by Dun Laoghaire Borough Council to make a "reservation" for the new road through the 71 acres of land at St Helen's, off the Stillorgan Road. The cost of this motorway link, including a bridge over the railway and an "interchange" on Merrion Strand, would be roughly £23 million for a "basic" road or up to £41 million for the "deluxe" model, built in a cut-and-cover tunnel to minimise environmental damage. What concerned conservationists was the fact that this road, in one form or another, would gouge its way through Booterstown Marsh, a long-established bird sanctuary and nature reserve which Dun Laoghaire Corporation supposedly had a policy to protect. Borough officials were undaunted, however. Incredibly, they argued that the road plan represented a "unique opportunity" to recreate the bird marsh on an alternative site, located between the DART line and the new road out on the strand. The fact that it took decades for the existing marsh to develop, after the original railway line to Kingstown was built in 1834, was studiously ignored. And the widespread opposition to the road scheme, among local residents and environmentalists alike, counted for little with a slim majority of the councillors when they agreed to reserve space for it.

On the northside, we can see another glimpse of the same road scheme in the draft city plan's proposed reservation of land for a "Drumcondra By-Pass", which would cut through Griffith Avenue destroying the grandest legacy to Dublin of 1920s town planning. Coincidentally, it follows almost exactly the same route, from Collins Avenue to Clonliffe Road, as the Eastern By-Pass defeated in 1980 by the City Council. This is not at all surprising, because Dublin Corporation's engineers had never accepted the council's decision as final and, within two years, they got consultants to produce an "Inner City Relief and Port Access Route", which was the Eastern By-Pass with a new name and some changes from the original plan. And though this scheme was never approved, the engineers kept harping on the need for an eastern crossing of the Liffey to "faciltate port traffic". Yet when it came to producing the draft city plan, neither the engineers nor the Corporation's senior management had the courage to put this supposedly vital road in the plan because of the renewed controversy it would provoke. Instead, with a fight already on their hands over the Inner Tangent and other road schemes, they decided to wait until the plan came back from public exhibition before attempting to reintroduce the Eastern By-Pass. And by dragging their feet over demands to sort out the traffic problems in hard-hit areas like Irishtown, they could even hope that it might actually win some support from local communities on this occasion.

More importantly, the engineers' plans have been endorsed by DKM, SKC and Reid McHugh in their consultancy study. "A Dublin Port Access Route, although it does not form part of the 1987 Draft Development Plan, is nonetheless a proposal of long standing", they say. "Without doubt it is probably the single most important strategic decision to be taken on transportation in Dublin. Very little progress can be made towards improving the environment of the Inner City or CBD until the significant volumes of extraneous traffic which currently pass through are much reduced. It was estimated that this could be 20,000 pcu's [pasenger car units] per day in addition to traffic generated by the Port. In particular, it is imperative that heavy commercial traffic bound for the Port through the CBD be substantially reduced. There does not appear to be any realistic alternative other than a new route to solve this problem''.

The consultants concede that the proposed "port access route" would "pass through areas of considerable environmental sensitivity" and, indeed, they say it was for this reason that the earlier Eastern By-Pass scheme was dropped from the city development plan in 1980. "One could question the correctness of this decision, but there is no doubt that the earlier version did lack a sufficient awareness of environmental effects. However, the real issue now is if an improved version could be designed which would deal adequately with the environmental problems. From a preliminary examination and discussions with Dublin Corporation, and without wishing to pre-empt the results of an Environmental Impact Study on the proposal, it is believed that by using part cut-and-fill tunnels and other expedients on an altered route, it should be possible to meet most of the previous objections''.

It is hard to share the consultants' confidence on this score. At the time of writing, no plans for the "port access route" had been published. However, it's already apparent that among the environmentally sensitive areas which will be directly affected are Booterstown Marsh, Merrion and Sandymount strands and Griffith Avenue. Cutting a tunnel through the marsh sufficiently large to carry up to six lanes of traffic would require major civil engineering works, on such a scale as to destroy the marsh itself. A "cut-and-cover" tunnel of equivalent size on Merrion and Sandymount strands would cause less long-term damage, but the use of this "expedient" would add enormously to the cost of the road project. And there seems to be no way around demolishing at least ten fine houses on Griffith Avenue, tunnel or no tunnel. What all of this illustrates is the open-ended nature of the commitment at the highest levels of Government to cater for private transport. Indeed, one of the justifications offered for the motorway along Sandymount Strand is that it would serve as a "Merrion Gates Relief Road" - in other words, it would overcome the problem of private cars having to queue on Merrion Road and Strand Road while the gates at the level crossing are closed to facilitate DART trains. And the provision of this new road could actually undermine the State's investment in DART if, as seems certain, it ends up being heavily-used by commuters.

There's no doubt, however, that catering for port traffic presents a genuine problem. The Liffey Quays, in particular, are rattled by an almost endless procession of juggernauts travelling between the port and the roads to the west. Until the early 1980s, the engineers had "long-term" plans to deal with this problem by setting back the building line along most of the quays to create a uniform road width of 60 feet. But since they rediscovered Colin Buchanan's 1962 idea of making "environmental precincts" in the city, which would be theoretically free of through-traffic, this destructive scheme could no longer be defended. Not all the quays have been reprieved, however. Ellis Quay, Ushers Quay and Ushers Island are still affected by road-widening schemes and, standing right in the path of a new bridge over the Liffey from Blackhall Place is the house where James Joyce set his most famous short story, *The Dead*. Arran Quay would also be hit by the demolition of the entire east side of Queen Street, destroying the architectural context of Queen Maeve's Bridge, the oldest on the river. The engineers had intended to pull down the entire west side of Queen Street, but they recently changed their plans. Now their sights are set on east side, and they want rid of a whole terrace of buildings to create a "filter lane for left-turning traffic" onto Arran Quay.

If there was a genuine desire to solve the problem of access to Dublin Port, as opposed to catering for commuters, the road planners would be examining other options. It has often been suggested that much more use could be made of the railway to carry freight to and from the port and, perhaps, a terminal outside the city where the containers could be picked up by the road vehicles. However, even if this could be done - and a subsidy would be required, as in Britain, to compensate for the extra costs involved - there would still be the problem of catering for "ro-ro" traffic, i.e. articulated trucks which drive on and off the ferries. At present, there are two separate railway lines running into Dublin Port. The road engineers would be doing the city a service by investigating the possibility of converting one of them - the one which runs from the North Wall alongside the Royal Canal and through a tunnel under the Phoenix Park - into a road exclusively reserved for port traffic, linking up with the Chapelizod by-pass and the Western Parkway. In this way, trucks from the port bound for the western outskirts of the city (where much Dublin's industry is now located) would be able to by-pass the centre - and the Liffey Quays, in particular. That, in turn, would be almost enough to assure the quays a future, especially as a place to live.

There is one thing standing in the way of such a solution: the EC study consultants suggest that this particular railway line should be used to provide a diesel train service between Clondalkin and Pearse Station, Westland Row. This closely reflects the Government's October 1987 statement, knocking any extension of the DART off the agenda and insisting, instead, that further improvements in public transport would be confined to buses and diesel rail services "on existing lines". As a result, the consultants propose no rail spur to Tallaght, despite the fact that a land reservation to accommodate it has been protected in successive county development plans. Instead, the 70,000 plus people who live there would have to rely on feeder bus services to take them to the new station in Clondalkin - a distance of up up five miles, in some cases. Yet the consultants concede that Tallaght is the "least well served" area in transportation terms, with peak-travel times for journeys to and from the city centre twice as long, on average, as the equivalent trip by DART. Their suggestion that this imbalance could be overcome by providing nothing more than a bus/rail service to improve city centre accessibility from Tallaght seems utterly improbable.

The road engineers argue that the city centre must be accessible in order to survive. Who could disagree? Obviously, city centre shops must be in a position to compete for custom with the many purpose built shopping centres in the suburbs - and, in this context, accessibility is clearly vital. However, an integrated rail-based system of public transport would make the city centre by far the most accessible location in the metropolitan area, for shoppers and commuters alike, without the need to transform streets into dual- carriage-ways. It is surely significant that the Dublin City Centre Business Association, which represents the main shopping interests in the central business district, is calling not for more road-widening schemes to facilitate cars as a priority, but for DART-type rail services linking the core of Dublin with the outer suburbs.

At present, the streets and roads of the inner city and inner suburbs are clogged with the cars of suburban commuters. Indeed, Dr Andrew MacLaran, lecturer in geography at Trinity College, insists that the centre of Dublin has been turned into a "massive car park". He was commenting on the findings of an on-the-spot survey carried out by 70 of his students in March 1989 which found that the chances of getting caught for illegal parking on the streets of the city centre were as low as one per cent. In the prime area, covering the CBD, where meter parking costs 60 pence an hour, the students discovered that 1,600 parked cars were breaking the law while only 1,056 were observing it. Yet only seven of the 820 cars parked on yellow lines between the hours of 10 am and 12 noon had received parking tickets, and just eight of the 463 cars illegally parked at meters had been ticketed. Similarly, in the secondary zone surrounding the CBD, where parking costs just 30 pence an hour, the survey found that 3,549 of the 7,920 cars parked there were "illegals", but only 23 of them had been caught by the traffic wardens. As Dr MacLaran said, what the survey points to is "the almost total absence of any attempt seriously to enforce parking regulations in the city, even in areas which have already witnessed widespread townscape destruction to improve the traffic flow". He added: "You are forced to ask yourself whether the city's traffic planners would prefer to waste vast sums of taxpayers' money on expensive, socially disruptive and environmentally destructive schemes, knocking down one side of a street to create an extra traffic lane, rather than see our road capacity used to its full potential''.

Indeed, the Trinity College survey underlines the fact that nothing much has changed on the city's streets since 1980, when the report from the Government-appointed Transport Consultative Commission (TCC) also concluded that illegal car parking was rampant in the centre of Dublin. If anything, the latest survey actually underestimates the full extent of the problem because it takes no account of the widespread incidence of off-street car parking on cleared sites - many of which are operating illegally, without planning permission. Here again, little or nothing is done to enforce the law, even in cases where permission has been refused. (The pressure for commuter car parking in the city centre has become so acute that some have made arrangements to rent extra space in church grounds in and around the central business district). And despite the fact that surface car parking has become a major economic use of land in the city centre, it would appear that these "temporary" car parks will not be covered by the new Derelict Sites Act, which means that the owners will not have to pay an annual levy based on each site's development value. Yet the proliferation of surface car parks in and around the city centre, by providing the capacity for car parking, merely encourages more commuters to drive into town, aggravating the congestion on arterial roads at peak-time. And it is this congestion which creates a perceived need for road-widening schemes to accommodate the additional traffic - even at the cost of demolishing much of the city's fabric. The city manager, Frank Feely, once defended the controvesial dual-carrigeway scheme for Patrick Street, New Street and Clanbrassil Street by saying that he knew how much these streets needed to be widened because his own car "stalls there every morning" on the way in from Templeogue. Thus, when the engineers presented him with their plans, he would instinctively have seen the point of it all.

The EC study consultants draw particular attention to the need for a crack-down on illegal parking in the city centre. "It is thought that, as a conservative estimate, a good enforcement system could give an effective 5% road network capacity increase", it says. "It is impossible, therefore, to make a case for expansion of road or junction capacity in the Inner City while the present standard of enforcement persists. This issue is so important that it ought to be a pre-condition for all future transportation investment in the Inner City. Enforcement is not alone highly cost-effective in terms of the time savings it can achieve and in terms of its impact on the modal split, but it would also result in significant environmental benefits". All alternatives, they say, "including a specialist traffic corps with the responsibility and accountability for enforce-ment", should be looked at to bring about the required degree of change. "Wheel-clamps, on-the-spot fines, tow-away vehicles and other expedients are needed in a determined effort to have traffic regulations taken seriously. These regulations are for the benefit of everyone and it is not in the public interest that the real cost of a breach of the law (defined by the amount of the fine multiplied by the probability of having to pay a fine) should be so low. Enforcement would also be helped by a set of coherent and understood measures, like off-street car parking, designed to avoid the need for traffic law violation. It also needs a sustained public relations effort".

Frankly, this is a laugh. It is like saying that we're all against sin and we want to see it stamped out. The truth, however, is that there is no consensus in this country on the need for rules and regulations of any kind about anything - least of about parking cars in cities and towns, which almost nobody takes seriously. The same problem was highlighted and the same strong recommendations were made in the 1980 TCC report - but little, if anything, was done to implement them. The Dublin Transport Authority was eventually set up, but with less teeth that the commission intended, and it was only in office for six months when the previous Government abolished it. And not incidentally, this decision was made soon after reports started to circulate suggesting that the DTA was about to introduce wheel-clamping for illegally parked cars. The gardai were also not sorry to see the DTA go. Its demise meant that they retained control over the traffic wardens; if the TCC's report had been implemented, they would have been transferred to the DTA. What chances are there that the latest solemn call for a crackdown on illegal parking is going to fall on anything but arid ground?

The availability of *ad lib* car parking in the city centre is crucial to the the whole debate on transport options. Indeed, the consultants say that parking policy is "potentially one of the most powerful planning intervention levers available for modal split adjustment" - i.e. altering the current imbalance between private and public transport. Noting that their relative positions have been reversed in 20 years, with 54 per cent of commuters using buses then to 52 per cent using cars now, they say: "An unbalanced modal split means too many commuters in the city centre, a poor public transport service, insufficient parking and congested roads. What ought to be its primary attractions as a location for retailing and business are lost".

Yet the credibility of the consultants' recommendations on tilting the modal spilt back in favour of public transport rests on a much stricter parking regime. This is particularly true of the propposed port access route, as they themselves concede. "Since a Port Access Route could also improve access for cars to the CBD it could, unless matched by some expedient to restrict cars in the CBD, be in conflict with objectives to alter the modal split in favour of public transport. Traffic management and enforcement are obviously very important in how they affect modal split to the CBD. All road and rail plans in addition must be looked at in this context". Significantly, however, when it comes to the Singapore-style concept of "road pricing" - i.e., charging commuters for driving their cars - the consultants stop well short of such a "radical new measure" on the grounds that it would prove to be "highly controversial". (The same would apply to any serious crackdown on illegal parking).

Former Taoiseach Garret FitzGerald, in his contribution to the Dail "debate" on the Government's National Development Plan, said he had been advocating the idea of road pricing for 20 years. "Parking controls alone will not effect the necessary adjustment between public and private transport", he declared. "The only way that can be done is by the private motorist being charged at peak hours a price for using road space commensurate with the actual cost of that road space in economic terms. The reason public transport has declined in Dublin is because the private sector is subsidised to an enormous extent. Road space is given free to private motorists, usually one person in a car, at a time when that road space has enormous value. They get it free. With that enormous subsidy from the community to them, naturally the facility is over-used. If champagne were free, it would be over-drunk. If a valuable product is made available free of charge, people will use it and abuse it to the point of the grossest economic disortion''.

But if there is no political will to tackle the parking problem, there is little sign either that politicians are prepared to invest in a transport system that would persuade motoring commuters to leave their cars at home. Apart from the electrification of the Howth-Bray suburban railway line, approved in 1979 at an eventual cost of £115 million, successive governments have shied away from any decision to commit substantial funding for public transport in Dublin - mainly because of the cost. It particularly horrifies the Department of Finance because, on top of the expense of installing a rail rapid transit system, there would be an open-ended commitment to subsidise the annual running costs. There is evidence, however, that the Department itself inflated the real cost of providing the DART by pocketing EC grants for the project and forcing CIE to borrow the money to make up the difference. This also explains why the annual deficit is so high - because the vast bulk of it is accounted for by interest payments on the debt. At the same time, an estimated £280 million is being invested in roads - including schemes which have had a devastating impact on the city, like the Parnell Street dual-carriageway - and nobody in power ever seems to ask how much all of this is really costing (interest charges included) now and in the future.

A DART-type rail network, serving the city and most of its suburbs, would be the ideal solution and, though the cost is officially regarded as excessive, it should be seen in the context of its wider social and environmental benefits to the city - and the enormous price being paid for the road plans. Dr P.J. Drudy, in his road costs study, estimates that in the period since 1980 the financial cost of road improvements, maintenance and the overheads associated with them in the Greater Dublin area exceeds the cost of providing a rail rapid transit system - and this is *before* environmental and other "social" costs are taken into account. But for those who believe that a full DART system would be too expensive, there are cheaper alternatives such as light rail transit which would travel on the surface, running on special reservations in the suburbs and then joining the street system in the city centre. This would, in effect, be an up-dated version of Dublin's old tram system, abandoned 40 years ago, but using articulated trams similar to those already operating with great success in many Continental cities. One could envisage such a line operating from Tallaght to Heuston Station (Kingsbridge) and then running along the entire length of the Liffey quays at least as far as Tara Street and, perhaps, even to Connolly Station in Amiens Street.

The EC study consultants firmly reject any extension of DART on the grounds that a high-capacity rapid rail system would be unsuited to what "is basically a low density city". They argue that the cost of providing even a basic system would outstrip the resources likely to be available for all forms of transportation and other economic measures in the Dublin area under the EC Structural Funds. Even then, they claim, the system "would probably cater for less than 10% of the total transport demand of the area. It would make no contribution to freight transport or to important questions of diverting through-traffic from the city centre". However, they add this important rider: "It should not be inferred that, in changed circumstances beyond the timescale of the [five-year] programme, DART or some form of light rail transit system would never be an option...At the same time, long-term plans for DART or some other system should not prevent low-cost solutions being implemented now".

As well as proposing a £31 million diesel rail service on existing lines to Clondalkin and Blanchardstown, the "low-cost solutions" favoured by the consultants consist largely of improving the bus services which, they say, already carry 9 out of 10 of all public transport users in Dublin and "are clearly a better target for investment", given the low-density nature of the city's suburbs. "Unless a very serious effort is made to assist the bus service increase its market share of commuter trips from 23% at present, there will always be a city centre transport problem", their report declares. "Busways and bus lanes should be used in all situations where it can be shown that they would assist the achievement of CBD access objectives without causing environmental difficulties or, in the case of bus lanes, being a waste of scarce urban road space. A Port Access Route should be so designed as to have special bus facilities, including exclusive access points, and any radial road improvement inside the motorway ring must be shown to assist bus traffic".

However, it must be regarded as very doubtful that buses can ever provide more than a partial solution to the transport problem. Unlike trams, they must compete for road space in the city with the rest of the traffic and, inevitably, this results in considerable delays for bus passengers. Some 60 bus lanes were introduced during the early 1980s, in that brief period when it seemed as if Dublin was starting to tackle the problem of traffic congestion, but most of these lanes covered only short stretches of road and whatever initial gains were made in journey times have been been more than offset by the delays associated with the arrival - 25 years on - of driver-only buses. But there is a perception among those who make decisions about Dublin that public transport is essentially for the poor; and indeed, businessmen in pin-striped suits are a rare sight on the buses. As other cities have discovered, only a rail-based system is capable of providing the fast, efficient and reliable service these and other commuters will require if they are to leave their cars at home.

The consultants endorse long-standing proposals for a £16 million busway on the old Harcourt Street railway line, initially as far as Dundrum but with the possibility of an extension to Leopardstown "when the first phase has proved itself". At the Harcourt Street end, they say, "it may be necessary to improve the links between Camden Street and Harcourt Street in order to facilitate a bus lane system". In relation to equally long-standing plans for a busway from Tallaght to the city centre, via Mount Argus, they suggest that this should be deferred in the short-term to see whether the cheaper alternative of providing feeder buses to Clondalkin station is working out. "A straight choice exists in the longer term between higher cost alternatives - namely, the Tallaght Busway and a rail spur to Tallaght Town Centre from the Clondalkin line'', their report declares. "In addition to proving the market for the latter by feeder bus services and further study, the practical and environmental difficulties of the proposed Tallaght Busway need to be studied in much greater depth". The consultants rightly identify the section from Harold's Cross Bridge to Kimmage as presenting "the main difficulty", and they say it would be "difficult to produce a design (for this stretch) without causing a lot of environmental problems".

But catering for the needs of public transport should not involve sacrificing another large chunk of the city centre to make way for a new central bus station, in association with a massive commercial development. That's what lay in store for the Temple Bar area until a vigorous campaign to defend it - plus the obvious appeal of its cobbled streets, historic buildings and lively "Left Bank" uses - persuaded the powers-that-be to locate the bus station elsewhere. Now this alternative site - the entire area bounded by Abbey Street and the Quays, Jervis Street and Bachelors Lane - is being "assembled" by Arlington Securities, a British property company, in collaboration with CIE. The plan provides for a vast underground car park accommodating 1,500 cars, a shopping centre at ground and first-floor levels which would be twice the size of the St Stephen's Green Centre and, astonishingly, a bus station on top. Long ramps would be required to bring the double-decker buses up to third-floor level and, at peak times, there would be up to 800 "bus movements" per hour between these ramps and the surrounding street system. Even John Prendergast, the manager of the Corporation's planning department, whose natural disposition - as he so often says himself - is to grant permission for development, has admitted that this would raise serious traffic and "civic design" problems.

Unless great sensitivity is shown by the designers, this scheme could also threaten the surviving buildings on Bachelors Walk and Ormond Quay, as well as most of those on Middle and Upper Abbey Street. Some of the Georgian houses on Bachelors Walk are among the earliest in Dublin, with superb wood-panelled interiors, but the retention of the remaining quay frontage is also essential to preserve the city's most memorable image - the view westwards from O'Connell Bridge. But even if all of the streetfront buildings are retained and the shopping centre/bus station is confined to the "backland" area behind them, the whole scheme would still have an enormous impact on the city centre. To cater for "bus movements" in and out of the bus station, it would almost certainly mean the closure of Lower Liffey Street as well the construction of a new bus-only bridge over the river, between Wellington Quay and Jervis Street and this, in turn, could mean routing buses from the southside through the Temple Bar area, via Eustace Street - an alarming prospect, if the area is to be sensitively conserved.

As originally conceived, the central bus station was to have been merely a part of a "transportation centre" incorporating a road/rail interchange. In other words, the city's buses would be at surface level, linked directly to an underground DART station on a new line between Heuston and Connolly. But this has now been scrapped, both by the Government and its consultants, so all we're left with is a bus station, and there must be considerable doubt about whether this would work on its own. In 1986, the Temple Bar Study Group argued not only against locating such a facility in that historic area but also against the concept itself. Their report suggested that it wouldn't work - especially in the absence of a rail interchange - and said the main reason why a central bus station was being supported by Dublin Corporation was that it would take bus termini off the streets, thus making more room for cars. But if a station really was required, the group proposed that it should be located on Irish Life's four-acre derelict site at George's Quay, right beside the DART line and just opposite the Custom House Docks site. Alternatively, they suggested that all buses should run through the city centre, to or from termini in the suburbs - much as the 10, 11, 16, 19 or 22 routes do already - thus eliminating the need to park what often seems like an army of buses on the main streets. But through-running would be more costly, in purely financial terms, and the Government has shown no willingness to increase the annual subsidy to Dublin Bus. Indeed, the company is so squeezed by budgetary constraints that it must recover 80 per cent of its operating costs from the fares box. In Paris, by contrast, over 70 per cent of the cost of running the city's public transport system is covered by subsidy. It's no wonder, therefore, that Dublin Bus is now caught in the classic spiral of decline, characterised by a fatal combination of falling passenger numbers, cutbacks in services, higher fares, more cutbacks, still fewer passengers and so on.

The DKM/SKC/Reid McHugh consultancy study endorses the proposed central bus station - but with reservations similar to those of Dublin Corporation's planners. The consultants say that the Bachelors Walk/ Ormond Quay site offers an opportunity to create 1,500 car-parking spaces and "it is very doubtful if an opportunity to (do so) at such a good location will ever arise again". They also argue that the provision of a bus station would help to improve the "poor image" of bus transport in Dublin, restoring confidence in the bus as a travel mode; it would facilitate the 30% of passengers who transfer from one route to another at peak times, as well as removing bus terminii from the streets, helping the city centre to compete against outlying suburban shopping centres and paving the way for the restoration of Temple Bar. However, they warn that the estimated cost - at £50 million - "is so expensive as to jeopardise the whole idea". Because of the substantial funds involved, they say "it is imperative that both the benefit and cost side of this proposal be looked at more closely. An environmental impact study must also look at its effect on adjacent streets, on traffic in the area and on existing buildings on the site". On balance, the consultants conclude that "it may be possible to derive a worthwhile proposal from this concept. However, it must be examined in greater depth before it can be a firm recommendation of the programme". The great danger is that, having skewed its priorities so heavily in favour of roads, the Government may put forward the bus station as a "sop" to public transport and the city will end up with a glorified bus ghetto - for that is all it would be - in and around Bachelors Walk.

In its National Development Plan, the Government has allocated £212 million for spending on roads in the Dublin area and £36 million for public transport. With a western by-pass as well as an eastern by-pass (the "port access route"), the city would be well on the way to getting the 70-mile-long "motorway box" envisaged in the 1971 Dublin Transportation Study (DTS) - *but without the public transport improvements it also recommended*. As a result, Dublin would be left with a two-tier transport system - a high-grade electric rail service (DART) serving the affluent areas around the Bay, a low-grade diesel service for the poorer western suburbs and buses for everywhere else. However, the goal of creating an effective public transport system for the entire city should not be cast aside, at the whim of one Government, and the county council should hold the reservations for the rail lines until another opportunity arises in the years to come. Hasty decisions in earlier times are now bitterly regretted - like the closure of the Howth Tram and the West Clare Railway, which would have become tremendous tourist attractions had they been allowed to survive.

"If Dublin is to be saved, the Government must re-order its spending priorities, allocating at least as much money for public transport as it has for roads. And if sufficient funds are not available for both, as they evidently are not, public transport should get the lion's share, with the road programme correspondingly reduced", said the Dublin Crisis Conference *Manifesto for the City*. "Other measures needed to improve the transportation picture and the city's total environment would include the designation of central Dublin as a pedestrian priority area, with the Corporation continuing its programme of re-paving the main shopping streets and other streets becoming more pedestrian-oriented through the use of wider pavements, cul de sacs etc; the establishment of a comprehensive system of cycle lanes and secure lock-ups to encourage the growing use of bicycles as a means of transport; the rigorous enforcement of parking regulations, with realistic fines, wheel-clamping and the impound-ment of offending vehicles, and the imposition of charges on commuters who needlessly bring their cars into the city centre on a scale that would reflect the true economic cost of this anti-social practice".

One of the real problems which has bedevilled the city over the past 20 years is that the road planners (Dublin Corporation) and the public transport planners (CIE) have insisted on pursuing their own mutually exclusive visions of the city, each side holding out for the totality of their own particular master plan while refusing to consider less costly and more modest alternatives. Indeed, the consultants in their study of Dublin note that there was "a great variety of transportation proposals in existence, each with its own proponents and detractors". Thus, the Corporation engineers would settle for nothing less than their complete road network while their opposite numbers in CIE would only countenance a comprehensive city- wide DART system. But the road lobby is in the ascendant now, as never before, and CIE's underemployed transport planners - unable to achieve their goals in Dublin - find themselves reduced to tendering for light rail transit schemes in British cities like Manchester.

Yet there has never been a public inquiry into the Corporation's road plans or their cost in social, economic and environmental terms. All we have had is a series of limited hearings on the compulsory purchase orders for properties standing in the path of a small section of the planned road network. The only serious review undertaken in recent years was by the EC study consultants. Noting the present conflict over transportation planning in the city, they say: "The programme for the Greater Dublin Area will in effect, by recommending particular proposals, adopt a position in this debate. One would expect the programme, because of the sizeable funds which could be available, to have a decisive medium-term effect in steering transportation policy in a particular direction". However, the consultants describe their own report as "a rationali-sation of *existing* plans" (emphasis added) and they acknowledge the need for a full-scale land use and transportation study of the Dublin area. Such an exercise would need to reassess the rationale, from a transportation viewpoint, for the proposed road network but also at the wider environmental implications - including the cost to the city of losing so much of its built fabric in the cause of catering for cars.

The bitter conflict over the proposed dual-carriageway for Patrick Street, New Street and Lower Clanbrassil Street is just a foretaste of what is in store if the Corporation continues to push through its plans - in the face of the consultants' report. There is not even a consensus within the Corporation itself on the 62 road schemes included in the draft City Development Plan; the engineers wanted more, the planners less, so what is being put forward is a compromise - and, like all compromises, it can hardly be regarded as holy writ, incapable of being challenged. The engineers are themselves divided into two camps - the "old guard" headed by Peter Kelleghan, the chief city and county roads engineer, and his deputy, Michael Sullivan, and the "young turks" who are prepared to consider less drastic solutions. But the strategy being pursued by the Corporation has been seriously called into question by the consultants, whose jaundiced view of inner city road proposals led them to recommend that most, if not all, of them should be dropped. And since there is no real urgency to proceed with these plans, the City Council should either drop them altogether or defer making any final decision at least until the Government's application for EC funding is determined. Instead, the council should take the opportunity afforded by the city plan review to declare, clearly and unambiguously, that it supports a "balanced transportation policy" for Dublin - with the emphasis on improving and facilitating public, as opposed to private, transport.

Demolition in Harcourt Terrace...only the front facade of the Regency centrepiece, of numbers 6 and 7 on the terrace, has been retained in redeveloping the site for offices and "town houses".
Designed by Burke - Kennedy, Doyle and Partners. (Photograph: The Irish Times)

3

Containing Suburban Sprawl

During the 1970s, Dublin was often said to be "the fastest-growing capital in Europe", as if that was something to be particularly proud of, and certainly the city's expansion over the past 25 years has been spectacular. But the vast new suburban areas created to accommodate the increase in population have been less than successful, in social or environmental terms. For the most part, they are featureless low-density housing estates with no historical reference points or sense of place. Once fine country houses were often the first casualties of suburban expansion and, indeed, so few survive in Co Dublin that they could almost be regarded as an endangered species. Even when older features are retained, they are usually treated in a throw-away manner - none more so than the portico of Kenure Park, all that remains of the Palmers' great mansion in Rush, which now stands as a bizarre monument (to the vandalism of Dublin County Council?) in the middle of a non-descript housing estate.

Worst of all were the "low-cost" housing schemes of the 1960s and 1970s. First, there was Ballymun, the classic "high rise, low density" system-built solution. Its seven 16-storey towers, named after the signatories of the 1916 Proclamation, and surrounding eight-storey spine blocks were sold to Neil Blaney, then Minister for Local Government, as a "quick fix" for Dublin's housing crisis. High-rise flats were all the rage in Britain at the time, and the concept of tall blocks standing in acres of "parkland" looked particularly attractive in 1964, at the height of the dangerous buildings scare when dozens of decaying Georgian tenements were being condemned and demolished. The brave new world of Ballymun was completed in 1969 - just as serious problems with similar developments in Britain were beginning to emerge. Only five years later, indeed, the British Labour Government announced that no more high-rise housing would be built there and, by the late 1970s, some of the worst examples were being demolished.

SAVING THE CITY

In the meantime, the housing authorities here had decided to try out a radically different solution - "low rise, high density", the very opposite to Ballymun. This produced Darndale, a large "estate" of two-storey houses grouped closely together around alleyways and couryards, off the Malahide Road. Yet again, the result was a disaster. Similar schemes had worked well in British "new towns", but the planners had failed to take into account the fact that working class families in Ireland tended to be much larger, with five or six children compared with two or three in Britain. Thus, Darndale became a claustrophobic pressure-cooker, made even more intolerable by multiple deprivation. But, like Ballymun, it took a determined campaign by community leaders to persuade the Corporation to begin making amends for all the years of neglect. The age-old view that anything is good enough for the working classes - even the flat-roofed boxes of Cherry Orchard and South Finglas, two more dreadful low-cost housing schemes - takes a long time to change.

Throughout Dublin's suburbs, even in middle class areas, one of the real problems is that the housing estates are designed more for cars than for people - especially the women and children who spend most of their days at home. Roads are too straight and too wide - wide enough, it has been said, to allow two fire engines to pass each other travelling in opposite directions at the same time. Roadside verges are a standard width, front gardens a standard length and there are no houses on corners - all intended to preserve the sight-lines of passing motorists. Thus, tens of thousands of people have been condemned to live in a straight-jacket designed for them by the roads engineers, with speedways instead of streets outside their homes. And because the suburbs were built at the extremely low density of eight or ten houses to the acre, so wasteful of prime agricultural land, this combined with the road standards to make for a boring, ultimately dispiriting environment.

The road standards so rigidly applied to Dublin's suburbs have been thoroughly discredited over the past ten years; indeed, the local authorities themselves no longer apply them to their own housing estates, though it is only in recent times that the Dublin County Council has agreed to show some flexibility in cases where private sector house-builders came up with more imaginative layouts. Yet the lack of any civic design in the suburban environment is evident almost everywhere - aggravated by the fact that only a small percentage of the housing is actually designed by qualified architects - and this merely serves to confirm the view that suburban standards are the very antithesis of urban living. Indeed, this impression is reinforced by the absence of such basic facilities as corner shops, cinemas, neighbourhood pubs or community centres. Even the town centres promised to give at least a commercial "heart" to places like Tallaght have yet to materialise.

The reason why, for example, there are few pubs other than out-sized drinking barns is that the existing licence-holders in Tallaght and other development areas combined to ensure that Co Dublin would remain classified as a rural district with no new pub permitted within a mile of an existing one. Incredibly, they were allowed to get away with this stroke and the appalling result is places like Embankment City and the Belgard Inn, with seating for up to 2,000 and all the "ambience" of an alcoholic hypermarket. There are no corner shops, either - the road engineers regard them as a traffic hazard - so most people are forced to walk or drive to some "neighbourhood shopping centre", generally an uncovered "mall" of single-storey shops with aluminium shutters and plastic signs set in a tarmacadam car park. Alternatively, in those working class estates not deemed to have sufficient "spending power" to warrant one of these "centres", a service of sorts is provided by mobile vans or pre-fab huts.

The suburbs were designed on the assumption that every family would own at least one car, and the fact that this has not happened has meant social isolation for certain groups of people, particularly women. Social segregation has occurred on a massive scale, primarily as a result of Dublin Corporation's housing policies but also reflecting a high degree of class prejudice among the populace at large. Vast estates of the same type of houses have also contributed to the blandness of the environment, since it results in an unbalanced community made up of families all of the one age group by effectively excluding non-nuclear family arrangements (e.g. single or elderly people). In Tallaght, where the population now exceeds 70,000, a frightening 50 per cent of the people living there are under the age of 19 and a third are under 10. Young families, many living at or near the poverty line, face long journeys - often involving two bus trips - to visit grandparents in other parts of the city, and an outing to Dollymount Strand, for example, would cost a family of five (two adults and three children) over £10 for transport alone.

The low-density nature of Dublin's suburban sprawl has also been used as an argument against the provision of DART-type rail rapid transit as the principal mode of transport between the "new towns" and the city centre. It is suggested that the suburbs would have had to develop at higher densities in close proximity to the railway lines to make a rail-based system viable. Yet the existing DART line, though it runs along the rim of Dublin Bay, still manages to provide a valuable service for its limited catchment area, where the densities are not much higher than they are in Tallaght, Clondalkin or Ballyfermot. And aside from a proper public transport system, low housing density in the new suburbs has also inhibited the provision of adequate, accessible support services; indeed, though Clondalkin is located beside the "city gate" of the natural gas pipeline from Kinsale, the combined effect of low housing densities and lower-than-average household income makes it relatively un-economic to install a gas grid in the area.

The western "new towns" of Tallaght, Blanchardstown and Lucan/Clondal-kin lack credibility, even in the minds of State agencies. Thus, when An Post was asked in 1983 what space it would require in the massive "town centre" planned for Blanchardstown, the response was that they could probably manage with the existing sub post office in the village. Of course, Dublin County Council could have given the new towns at least a veneer of credibility by opening up development offices in each area, with its own planners operating on the ground. But all of the planning is done by remote control, from the Irish Life Centre in Lower Abbey Street, and in any case it is doubtful if any of the planners themselves actually live in the new towns they are helping to create. Some of them still maintain that, in years to come, these raw housing areas will develop a sense of place. But others will admit that because of the way they were designed, laid out and built, they haven't got the raw material from which a sense of place might be fashioned. Indeed, not even Patrick Shaffrey's imaginative idea of planting one million trees would cover up these basic defects.

As it is, the provision of open space in the new suburbs has been seen in quantitative rather than qualitative terms. So long as each estate fulfilled the minimum 10 per cent required, it received planning approval and the question of where to locate such open space was left to the developer. More often than not, this has resulted in a single tract of open space being provided - whatever useless bit of land happens to be left over after all the houses are built. Usually, this space is not overlooked, which means that it is of little benefit to most residents and can also end up being used as a venue for cider parties and other undesirable social activities. In the Hartstown area of Blanchardstown, the

Contrasting environments... 19th century terraced houses in the inner city (above) and, below, terraced suburban "starter homes" from the 1980s. State housing subsidies and stamp duties mean that young first-time house purchasers don't have a free choice about where, or what, to buy. (Photographs: The Irish Times).

As far as the eye can see... typical semi-detached suburban housing in Tallaght, Co. Dublin. Note the rectangular road grid, the random nature of the open space and the absence of houses facing corners. (Photograph: The Irish Times).

principal landscape "feature" of the public open space is a huge ESB pylon carrying a 220-kv power line. But then, this is an estate built by Dublin Corporation for its own tenants, and anything is good enough for the working classes. In general, however, it would be much better - both from a visual and practical point of view - if open space in housing estates was provided in several smaller overlooked units rather than one large tract, and without such extraordinary intrusions as 220-kv pylons.

But the greatest tragedy about the three "new towns" - now far too late to put right - is that they are in the wrong place. When Myles Wright, the British town planner, published his "advisory plan" for the Dublin region in 1967, the planning authorities - and the Government - simply ignored strong appeals from commentators like Uinseann MacEoin that residential development should be concentrated along the coastal railway line, from Balbriggan and Bray, which would at least have provided for transportation needs. Even Wright's preferred strategy, to create four "fingers" stretching westwards from the city, but separated from it, was not adopted. Instead, they became three big blobs, with Lucan and Clondalkin - two villages with identifiable centres - incongruously forced together because the local authorities, in a series of discreet deals, had bought up most of the land in between. Otherwise, what could and couldn't be built, where and when, was largely determined by the location of sewerage pipes. No wonder it is said that Co Dublin was "designed around drains".

In Britain, the first step to be taken in any "new town" scheme would be that all of the land required would be designated by an Act of Parliament and then taken into public ownership, at prices often not much more than its existing value as agricultural land. This, together with the establishment of a special commission to oversee the enterprise, gave planners effective control over the design, layout and scheduling of the entire development, with land being released in stages to the private sector for approved housing or industrial schemes. No such commission was established for Tallaght or the other "new towns" of Lucan/Clondalkin or Blanchardstown, perhaps because of our over-weening respect for the rights of private property or, perhaps, because the Government never took the matter seriously enough. The EC study consultants conclude that the absence of an overall development agency, with specific powers and functions and with a designated budget to oversee the implementation of the strategy was "a major weakness". What happened, therefore, was little better than *laissez faire* planning, hardly planning at all. Colours were inked on a map and, at the stroke of someone's pen, the landowners in possession of parcels zoned for development made a fortune. And if some found themselves on the wrong side of the lines drawn by the planners, they could always enlist the support of friendly county councillors to have their land rezoned.

Indeed, before the first County Development Plan was adopted in 1972, Dublin had experienced its first land rezoning scandal. Councillors, in both Fianna Fail and Fine Gael, combined to push through the rezoning of land which had never been earmarked for development, riding roughshod over the objections of the council's professional staff. This was particularly prevalent in the Swords area, where so much land never intended for development was rezoned that the original plan for a motorway to Belfast had to be scrapped; instead of following the route of the Swords by-pass, which was constricted in width because of all the unplanned housing built on both sides of it, the motorway will - at huge additional public expense - now run much further east of the town.

One of those responsible for this situation is Fianna Fail's Ray Burke, who as well as being a councillor was also an auctioneer with an intimate knowledge of land values in the north county area. In July 1974, after *Hibernia* and the *Sunday Independent* ran detailed stories exposing various land deals, the then Attorney General, Declan Costello, asked the gardai to carry out an investigation. A Garda report was made but no further action was taken. Reporter Joe McAnthony of the *Sunday Independent* had focussed in particular on Mr Burke's relationship with the Brennan and McGowan housebuilding group. As an auctioneer, he was the agent for the hundreds of houses they built in the Swords area. As a councillor, he tabled motions to have agricultural land which they had bought rezoned for development, immeasurably increasing its value. An extract from the accounts of one of the Brennan and McGowan companies - published by the newspaper - showed that he was to receive a sum of £15,000 in fees under the heading "Planning" in relation to the sale of 35 acres of newly zoned industrial land at Mountgorry, near Swords. Another Brennan and McGowan company built his house, "Briargate", on its own grounds off the Malahide Road. It was designed by the group's principal architect, John P. Keenan, who was later appointed as a member of Bord Pleanala by Mr Burke on his last day in office as Minister for the Environment, in June 1981. Mr Burke insisted that there was no connection between the motion he seconded to rezone the Mountgorry land for industry and the £15,000 payment. He also told the *Sunday Independent* that the sale of the land, to which the payment was linked, had not gone through.

It was not until 1979 that the the county council began considering its review of the County Development Plan. But instead of serving as a serious review of planning policies, this process merely opened the floodgates for another tide of applications from landowners to have their particular pieces of land rezoned for development. Altogether, before the draft plan went on public exhibition late in 1982, the councillors had chosen to ignore the repeated advice of their own planning officials and voted to rezone a total of 3,000 acres of land. Prominent for the roles they played in this affair were Larry McMahon (FG), Sean Walsh (FF), chairman of the council in 1988/89, and Jim Fay (FG), who held the first three places on a list of the "top ten rezoners", compiled by *The Irish Times*. But the public reaction was so critical that the council received over 4,500 objections from concerned citizens, and Mr McMahon as well as Liam Lawlor (FF), whose land in Lucan had been proposed for rezoning, lost their Dail seats in the November 1982 general election, largely because of all the adverse publicity. The Coalition Government intervened in the controversy and the then Minister for the Environment, Labour's Dick Spring, made it clear that rezoning decisions did not entail any commitment by the State to service the land in question. Quite separately, pressure was applied by the then Taoiseach, Garret FitzGerald, on Fine Gael councillors not to approve rezoning decisions taken against the advice of the planners. As a result, almost 80 per cent of these decisions were reversed before the County Development Plan was finally adopted in April 1983.

But it wasn't long until the planners also seemed to lose their heads. In April 1985, they produced their own updated version of the Myles Wright plan - the Eastern Region Settlement Strategy 2011 - which mapped out a 25-year plan, grounded on a projection that the population of the eastern region (Co Dublin along with Meath, Kildare and Wicklow) would increase by over half-a-million by the year 2011. To accommodate this large number of additional people, the ERDO strategists proposed more of the same type of suburban sprawl we have seen over the past 25 years while, at the same time, discounting the possibility of accommodating even an extra 10,000 people in the inner city. The bulk of the projected population increase was to be located in the Dublin sub-region, in areas on the periphery of suburban "dormitory towns", with - for example - a "major urban complex" housing an extra 130,000 people, in the Swords/Donabate area. However, the ERDO report's projections were seriously undermined by the 1986 census, which showed a significant falling-off in the rate of population growth - as a result of later marriages, smaller family sizes and emigration - and the Coalition Government soon sent its authors back to the drawing-board.

They produced a revised strategy in May 1988, but this was basically just a scaled-down version of the earlier report - with the emphasis again on peripheral expansion and still no great hopes for a resurgence of interest in the inner city. It projected having to cater for an extra 225,000 people in the eastern region by the year 2001, though this must be regarded as wildly optimistic given the continuing high levels of emigration. "The probability is that this population increase will not be reached, but the possibility remains that it could be exceeded", the ERDO strategists said, hedging their bets. So, just to be on the safe side, they recommended that more land should be zoned for residential development - mainly in peripheral areas south and west of the city. Yet again, they seem to have ignored the growing trend towards developing infill sites closer to the city centre. And as for housing in the centre, the planners said the prospects "appear bleak" - unless there was a concerted effort to create a market for it. But even before the report was published, it had been accepted by the board of the Eastern Regional Development Organisation - their last act before being wound up - and its recommendations will probably be implemented, in one way or another.

As the *Manifesto for the City* pointed out, one of the most fundamental objections to the ERDO strategy - in its original and revised forms - is that the study on which it is based was carried out in the absence of any national policy on the location of population and economic activity, and it contains little or no reference to what is happening or what is likely to happen elsewhere. "What is now required is a national settlement strategy which specifies clearly the targets for population and employment in the various regions with the aim of taking some of the pressure off Dublin. Indeed, in view of the Dublin sub-region's inability so far to accommodate population growth in an orderly manner, every effort must be made to discourage in-migration from other regions - and even to encourage some people living in the Dublin area to relocate elsewhere by providing sufficiently attractive 'counter magnets' in provincial cities like Cork, Limerick, Galway and Waterford.

"Such a statement of targets would have widespread implications for future investment in housing, schools, roads and other infrastructure, and it must be guided by a policy of urban consolidation - in other words, that resources would be allocated to Dublin and the main provincial cities to rebuild derelict inner areas with a mix of housing, shops, offices and small industry, thus counteracting the relentless drift towards the periphery and beyond", the manifesto declared. In this context, it should be remembered that ERDO's disastrous projection of Dublin's inner city as the lifeless hub of a sprawling conurbation was based on the crudest of calculations. Because what the authors of the strategy did was to take a typical three-bedroom house and work out how much it would cost to build it in the inner city, as opposed to a "greenfield" site in the suburbs. And when they found that the former would cost considerably more than the latter, they concluded that there was "not a good case" to be made for the inner city as a residential prospect. However, in reaching this conclusion, they took little or no account of the value of surviving inner city shops, schools, social services and amenities or the enormous costs to the community of providing similar facilities in the suburbs.

The EC study consultants, in their report, say the desirability of encouraging large-scale private residential development in the inner city "raises a number of issues" about the present settlement strategy for the Dublin area. "Given the huge investment in services and the desirability of the new western towns achieving a 'critical mass' capable of sustaining a full range of facilities and amenities, additional residential developments are required, especially in Lucan/Clondalkin and Blanchardstown. At the same time, it must be recognised that the house-building industry is increasingly targeting infill sites in developed suburbs, reflecting a shift in demand from starter units to houses for the trading-up sector", they say. "There are also doubts about the capacity of the authorities to direct residential development to particular areas when there is no shortage of serviced land throughout the sub-region. Finally, account must be taken of the slowdown in net household formation in recent years. In the circumstances, and particularly if new private residential development is to be encouraged in the Inner City, the implications for the western towns need to be considered, as the prospects for further residential development there are very poor. Public policies must reflect the fact that these areas may never achieve the 'critical mass' as planned".

The consultants note that Tallaght, with its population now exceeding 70,000, is the fourth largest settlement in Ireland, roughly on a par with Limerick. "Although Tallaght might seem to be within striking distance of achieving 'critical mass' in terms of securing a range of higher order functions and services (such as a town centre, hospital and third-level college), the rate of development there has slowed dramatically in recent years", they say. "Current annual rates of completion [for new housing] are only about one-quarter of the annual rate in the early 1980s in all three western development areas. If the present rate of of construction [1986-88] were to persist, there is enough fully-serviced residential land in Tallaght to last a further 30 years. If the same arguments are applied to Lucan/ Clondalkin and Blanchardstown, there is enough fully-serviced residential land to last 36 years and 70 years, respectively. Clearly, there is little prospect of either Lucan/Clondalkin or Blanchardstown achieving 'critical mass' as autonomous development areas over the next 10 years".

This pessimistic conclusion was confirmed in April 1989 by a survey of house prices which showed that, in spite of the property boom elsewhere in the city, houses built during the 1970s in the three western "new towns" had actually *fallen* in value over the previous three months. And one of the main reasons cited by estate agents for this negative trend was that poor infrastructure had made these areas less attractive. The consultants also say that the western development areas have been "starved of investment to fund necessary social and economic infrastructure". At the same time, however, they say there has been "substantial over-investment in the provision of serviced land in the light of recent and prospective population trends". They illustrate this neatly by suggesting that the "starkest fact" in relation to housing development in the three western development areas is that Dublin Corporation has some 1,200 acres of undeveloped fully-serviced land for housing, "for which there is no prospective demand in the forseeable future". Dublin County Council's undeveloped, but fully-serviced, land bank for housing in the same areas amounts to about 600 acres.

Yet month by month, Dublin county councillors vote to re-zone more and more land elsewhere in the county for suburban development, using the devices of "Section 4" motions and "material contraventions" of the County Development Plan, and it looks as if there will be a repetition of the earlier scandals when they get around to "reviewing" the plan. A total of 45 contraventions of the county plan were passed by the council between September 1985 and May 1988, according to information elicited by Joan Maher, a Fine Gael councillor. Of these, 21 were contentious and were only adopted after a vote - more often than not, with the Fianna Fail majority solidly in support of changing the plan, even against official advice. An analysis of the record shows that Sean Walsh (FF) proposed or seconded nine of these contentious motions, followed by Liam Lawlor (FF) with five to his credit, and Cyril Gallagher (FF), Jim Gilbride (FF) and Jim Barry (FF), with three motions each. Meanwhile, the planners themselves remain stubbornly committed to completing the three western "new towns" to their "population design standard" - a foolhardy objective in the face of demographic trends and the mounting evidence that many Dubliners used to living in central areas do not want to be dumped far away from the city in bleak, featureless housing estates like Neilstown or Fettercairn. The area most in demand among Corporation tenants is the inner city and, even in the private sector, a large proportion of house-building activity - as the EC study consultants note - is now concentrated on "infill" sites within easy reach of the centre.

In Belfast, the recent resurgence of interest in inner city housing development is at least partly due to the fact that a "stopline" was drawn around the city in the 1960s, with the intention of putting a brake on suburban development. Instead of embarking on another round of the land rezoning scandal, Dublin County Council should consider implementing this rough translation, in planning terms, of Parnell's famous phrase - "Thus far shalt thou go and no further". And they could begin by de-zoning the substantial tract of undeveloped land between Lucan and Clondalkin, thereby creating an instant green belt and restoring the individual identities of these towns.

But measures are also needed to improve the quality of life for people who will end up living in the suburbs. These should include the adoption of higher housing densities, such as those which apply to some of the much-praised Corporation housing schemes in the city, with the aim of creating a more intimate, neighbourhood-like environment. (The present standard density of eight to ten houses per acre, incidentally, is based on the Garden City movement's notion that each family would need a minimum of half a rood to grow enough vegetables to feed themselves - if they worked hard enough at it). Housing layout guidelines also need to be brought fully into line with the concepts outlined in Foras Forbartha's booklet "Streets for Living", with the emphasis on narrower road widths, cul-de-sac developments, the separation of pedestrian and motor traffic as far as possible, and the loosening of standard lengths for front and back gardens.

Equally vital is the need, sooner rather than later, to take the "green belt" areas into public ownership or control, averting the dreadful prospect that much of the western perimeter of the city could be transformed into a continuous "concrete jungle". Much of this land remains in private hands - some of it being held for speculative gain - and past experience has shown that it is seriously threatened by rezoning and compensation claims; indeed, this is already happening. One possibility which could be considered is the designation of the green belts as areas of special amenity, within which private farming would be encouraged, though public ownership may, in the end, be the only effective guarantee that the green belts will survive. Similarly, if the priceless amenity of the Dublin Mountains is to remain for succeeding generations to enjoy, a Special Amenity Area Order (SAAO) will have to be made to control undesirable developments in the mountain zone.

One of the main advantages of an SAAO is that, when adopted, it precludes compensation claims from landowners in the area covered by the order. However, there has been an enormous reluctance on the part of successive governments to contemplate the use of SAAOs even though the statutory provision has existed since the 1963 Planning Act. An order designed to protect the amenities of Dublin Bay languished in the Department of the Environment for almost four years before being turned down finally on the grounds that it was poorly drafted. More recently, Dublin County Council was encouraged by John Boland, during his brief but busy tenure as Minister for the Environment in 1986, to make an SAAO for the Liffey Valley. A public inquiry was held in September 1987 to give landowners in the area an opportunity to voice their objections, and the report of the inspector was delivered to the Minister for the Environment, Padraig Flynn, in January 1988. But at the time of writing, 18 months later, the Minister had still not made a decision on the matter. In the meantime, his Fianna Fail party colleagues on Dublin County Council, with Liam Lawlor TD to the fore, had whipped through a "material contravention" of the county plan to allow Bovale Developments Ltd - controlled by Mayo-born brothers Michael and Thomas Bailey - to build nearly 100 houses at Riversdale, on the Palmerstown side of the Liffey Valley, in return for the gift of 22 acres as a public amenity. Indeed, such *"quid proquo"* deals between developers and the local authorities have become an increasingly common feature of planning in Dublin.

But the whole issue of compensation will have to be tackled because it represents a fundamental obstacle to planning. This was thrown into sharp relief in March 1989 by Dublin County Council's defiance of a Supreme Court order to pay almost £1.9 million to Grange Developments and the High Court's unprecedented decision to put the council into receivership until the money was paid - which it was, within a matter of hours. The Grange case is extraordinary for another reason - it was the very first time, since the 1963 Planning Act came into force, that any local authority in the Republic actually had to pay a substantial sum in compensation to property developers over a refusal of planning permission. And it only happened because of the fact that attempts by county council officials to head off Grange's claim in the time- honoured fashion, by giving "undertakings" to grant permission for a variety of developments on the company's land at Mountgorry near Swords - the same land that Ray Burke helped to have rezoned - were found to be invalid by the courts.

There was bitter irony in the fact that a company controlled by Mayo-born property developers Tom Brennan and Joe McGowan was the beneficiary of the largest-ever payment of planning compensation. For Dublin County Council had been involved in more litigation with them over the years than with any other developer for breaches of the planning code relating to unfinished housing estates. Most notorious was Kilnamanagh, in the Tallaght area, which was supposed to be a "landscaped garden suburb" with 1,600 houses, plenty of open space and even "play lots" for the children. As their own advertisements put it, when the scheme was launched in 1973: "When you buy a home at Kilnamanagh, you get more than just a nice home. You buy a whole community - shops, supermarkets, bank, pub, garage, schools, churches, a community club and 50 acres of open space". By 1979, however, county councillors were calling for an inquiry into the "mess" which had been created in Kilnamanagh. It was just one huge unfinished housing estate, and the unfortunate residents had to resort to picketing showhouses and taking legal proceedings in a desperate effort to force the builders to meet their legal obligations. Apart from the fact that roads were left unsurfaced and other external services were not provided, some of the houses were found to be faulty and the much-heralded open space was often little more than a spoil heap for builders' rubble.

SAVING THE CITY

What most angered county councillors, however, was that there seemed to be no way of taking action against Brennan and McGowan by denying them planning permission for other housing schemes until the "mess" at Kilnamanagh had been put right. Like most large builders, they operated through a myriad of front companies, each one set up to carry out a specific development and forming a distinct legal entity. By the mid-1970s, Brennan and McGowan had become the biggest house builders in Ireland, turning out new houses at the phenomenal rate of up to 700 a year and far outstripping the output of established builders like McInerneys. In December 1983, their combined assets were valued at £11 million. By that stage, both of them had acquired stud farms - Mr McGowan buying Hollywoodrath, former home of the legendary Matt Gallagher, near Mulhuddart, and Mr Brennan opting for Hilltown Stud, near Clonee, Co. Meath. Two years later, in December 1985, counsel for a Dublin solicitor seeking redress against the two builders claimed in the High Court that their assets were being "dissipated at an alarming rate". The most recent statement had put the assets of one of them at just £608,000 and recorded a net liability in respect of the other.

Coincidentally, just one week before Grange exacted payment of its £1.9 million compensation award in March 1989, Mr McGowan sold Hollywoodrath for £1.5 million. Mr Brennan, meanwhile, retains an interest in Bardun Estates Ltd, which is pursuing another £2 million compensation claim against Dublin County Council over a refusal of permission for a housing scheme at Fortunestown, in Tallaght. And as in the Grange case, it was a decision by Bord Pleanala signed in March 1983 by Daniel Molloy - one of Ray Burke's appointees - that left the county council open to the claim. Another Bord Pleanala decision in March 1984, just 11 days before the Fianna Fail-appointed board was removed from office, paved the way for a Brennan and McGowan company called Criteria Developments Ltd to sell the Plantation site on Herbert Street, in the city centre, to John Corcoran's Green Property Company. The company's plan for an office development and block of flats on this choice wooded site, in the much sought-after southside Georgian core area, had been firmly turned down by Dublin Corporation's planners on amenity and other grounds. However, in a decision which conservationists at the time regarded as inexplicable, Bord Pleanala granted permission, subject only to the condition that some of the trees on the site should be preserved. It was signed by Anthony Lambert who had been Ray Burke's full-time constituency advisor until his boss appointed him to the planning appeals board in November 1982, on his last day in office as Minister for the Environment.

Almost single-handedly, Mr. Burke had undermined public confidence in the impartiality of the planning process by his last-minute appointments to Bord Pleanala after Fianna Fail's defeat in the general elections of June, 1981, and November 1982. On the first occasion, just hours before Garret FitzGerald's first government took office, he named three new members to the appeals board - John P. Keenan, principal architect for Brennan and McGowan, Daniel Molloy a Belfast-born businessman and Michael Cooke, a bye-law inspector with Dublin County Council, who had worked as a quantity surveyor for Brennan and McGowan. Later, during the interregnum between Fianna Fail's defeat in November, 1982, and another FitzGerald-led Coalition government taking office, Mr Burke named two more members to the board - Patrick Malone, Fianna Fail's director of elections in Laois-Offaly, and his own constituency advisor, Mr Lambert, a one-time travelling salesman. Pointedly, he declined to continue the tradition of appointing a senior official from the planning division of the Department of the Environment. Mr Burke justified his appointments on the basis that they would help to clear the backlog of appeals, but the Irish Planning Institute pointed out that what was really needed was more planning inspectors rather than new board members. Dick Spring, who took over as Tanaiste and Minister for the Environment in December 1982, also believed that Bord Pleanala -which was set up in 1977 to "take politics out of planning" - had suffered a major setback, and he was determined to do something about it.

Mr Spring decided to "reconstitute" the board, removing the Fianna Fail appointees from office and setting up an elaborate procedure for the appointment of board members at arm's length from the Government. In future, the chairman would be selected from among those recommended by a committee consisting of the President of the High Court, the secretary and chief engineering officer of the Department of the Environment, the chairman of An Taisce, the president of the Construction Industry Federation and the president of the Irish Congress of Trade Unions. There would be five ordinary board members - one a serving official of the Department and the other four selected from a list of nominees submitted by 22 bodies representing the professional, conservation, development and community interests in planning. In short, Bord

Pleanala was to be "depoliticised". But when Mr Spring produced his Bill in 1983 there was an outcry from Fianna Fail. The party leader, Mr Haughey described it as a "loathsome piece of politically-motivated legislation to try to assert some mean vindictive party political policy". He even led Fianna Fail deputies out of the Dail in protest after "the most unruly scenes seen in the chamber for many years", according to an *Irish Times* report. During the Dail debate, which was guillotined by the Government, Ray Burke said the "clear innuendo" in the Bill was that some members of Bord Pleanala were corrupt. "I stand over every appointment I made because they are decent and honourable men capable of carrying out their tasks", he declared. "I find it nauseating that a Government should, by innuendo, try to cast doubts on the decency and honour of members appointed by a previous administration". Padraig Flynn put it more colourfully, as usual : "The only sin they have committed is that they have stroked for Fianna Fail on ballot papers for a number of years". And he accused Mr Spring of giving the officials in his Department a one-sentance instruction - "sack those Fianna Fail hacks as quickly as possible and put a script in my hand that might make it seem plausible".

Seven board members, led by retired High Court judge George Murnaghan, sued the Government, claiming that their effective dismissal was contrary to natural justice. The action was settled out of court, apparently after they received undertakings that compensation equivalent to the salaries for their unexpired terms of office would be paid - in all, around £250,000. (Tony Lambert reverted to being Ray Burke's full-time constituency advisor, but he was taken back on the public payroll to work in Mr Burke's private office, first in the Department of Energy and, more recently, in the Communications and Justice departments). The first chairman of the "reconstituted" Bord Pleanala was Frank Benson, a former Corporation planner and executive director of Power Securities, the property developers, who later became chairman of the Custom House Docks Development Authority. The board is still being criticised for its decisions, by conservationists and developers alike, but the planning inspectors reports on which these are based remain confidential, so the public can't tell whether or not it is behaving capriciously. Recently, there have been calls from Dublin county councillors for a judicial inquiry into the board's affairs after the wording of a number of decisions to refuse planning permission - including the Bardun Estates case - left the council open to claims for compensation. Sean Lucey, the board's current chairman, said he did not believe that such an inquiry was necessary, but it would not worry him if one was held. The important thing, he said, was for people to recognise the impartial role of Bord Pleanala in adjudicating on planning appeals and ensuring "fair play". At the time of writing, the Gardai were carrying out an investigation into bribery allegations, on which the board felt it would be inappropriate to comment.

Whatever about the role of Bord Pleanala, it is abundantly clear that the fear of compensation claims has severely hampered the local authorities in fulfilling their statutory duty to secure the "proper planning and development" of their areas. The fact that such a derisory amount has actually been paid out in compensation claims over the past 25 years - in the case of Dublin Corporation, one of the largest local authorities, the total is less than £150,000 - merely indicates the extent to which the planning authorities have caved in under pressure. It also underlines the degree to which the threat of compensation has been used by developers as a "big stick" to browbeat the planning authorities, forcing them to grant permission for schemes which would otherwise have been refused for sound planning reasons. Not surprisingly, the vested interests - notably including the owners of land - find the existing arrangements quite congenial and this, more than any other factor, explains the reluctance of successive governments to tackle the compensation issue.

Yet the anomalies in the existing legislation have been evident for years. As far back as 1976, in the case of Viscount Securities v. Dublin County Council, the High Court construed from the 1963 Planning Act that a proposal to develop agricultural land as a housing estate would not involve a material change in the use of that land - a bizarre ruling that seemed to fly in the face of common sense. Then, there was the Supreme Court judgment, in the case of Nora Shortt v. Dublin County Council, which held that the plaintiff was entitled to full development value for her land because there was a sewer running through it - even though the land was zoned for part of the Dodder Valley linear park and the sewer was required to serve development areas like Tallaght. But despite the fact that the Department of the Environment was informed of this judgment on the very day it was made, and must have known that it would effectively prevent local authorities acquiring land for amenity purposes, a full five years passed before amending legislation was produced. This is in marked contrast to the alacrity with which governments have responded to court decisions in other areas, sometimes even rushing new legislation through the Dail in a single day.

Before the 1987 general election, Fianna Fail - in common with other political parties - promised that they would amend the 1963 Act so that the zoning of land would become a "non-compensatable" reason for refusing planning permission. In other words, if a particular piece of land was zoned agricultural, the landowner would no longer be able to claim compensation based on its value for, say, a housing estate. But when the Government's Planning Compensation Bill eventually emerged, it transpired that this crucial provision would only apply to land acquired after the date on which it was published - October 20th, 1988. And it wouldn't even apply to all land bought after that date. Land acquired by inheritance or as part of a "family settlement" would continue to be exempt, leaving open the possibility of landowners in these categories claiming compensation at any time in the future.

As the Irish Planning Institute (IPI) pointed out, the effect of these exclusions was such that the Bill would not reduce to any significant degree the eligibility of landowners to claim compensation. And having regard to the nature of land ownership on the fringes of Irish cities and towns - where compensation claims generally occur - the institute said the Bill would have no effect on family farms or on the long-term "land banks" held by development companies. In such cases, ownership would remain unchanged - thus staying outside the provisions of the Bill. Indeed, it would be possible for these landowners to apply for planning permission before selling their land and, if they are refused, they would be able to claim its full development value in compensation. Alternatively, they could avoid the provisions of the Bill by vesting title to the land in a limited company, later using the device of selling shares in the company to dispose of it. Thus, instead of being clear, simple and watertight, the Bill was so riddled with loopholes that landowners and their lawyers would continue to have a field day in the courts. In what he described as a "substantial" response to these concerns, the Minister for the Environment, Padraig Flynn, later tabled a series of amendments to close some of the loopholes - for example, by limiting the inheritance exemption to a period of 12 months after the Bill is enacted, but he continued the controversial cut-off date of October 20th, 1988, for all landowners already "in possession".

The IPI has argued, with some force, that local authorities should be able to refuse planning permission for any development which does not comply with the zoning objectives spelled out in their own Development Plans, without running the risk of claims for compensation. It pointed out that city and county development plans are reviewed every five years or so in a democratic process involving the citizens and their elected representatives. Everyone - including a landowner who is unhappy about the zoning of his land - can object, and their views must be taken into account before the plan is finally adopted. As the planners see it, the Development Plan - by providing a framework to regulate physical planning in each area - represents "the embodiment of the common good". Its use, therefore, as a measure of eligibility to claim compensation would be the most equitable way of regulating private property rights in accordance with "the exigencies of the common good" (to borrow a famous phrase from the Constitution).

For years, successive governments of all political hues have shied away from tackling the compensation issue, apparently because of a fear that any serious reform might be declared unconstitutional. Yet, in the case of XJS Investments v Dun Laoghaire Corporation, Mr Justice Niall McCarthy of the Supreme Court cast some doubt upon the constitutionality of a law (the 1963 Planning Act) which allowed property companies to claim large sums in compensation for planning refusals. The Constitution does guarantee the right to own private property, but Article 43 says this "ought in civil society to be regulated by the principles of social justice" and it declares that the State may "delimit by law" the exercise of private property rights "with a view to reconciling their exercise with the exigencies of the common good". The courts have so far been reluctant to offer clear interpretations of what this actually means and, indeed, judges have said more than once that this is more properly a matter for the Oireachtas. But given that Dublin County Council is now challenging the constitutionality of planning compensation, the courts may end up leading the legislators - just as they have done so often before.

The other issue intimately linked with the compensation problem is the whole matter of how land is valued. This has been governed by the ambiguous provisions of the 1963 Planning Act, under which landowners are allowed to have their claims for compensation assessed on the basis of the potential, rather than the actual, loss resulting from a refusal of planning permission. As a result, a property speculator may purchase agricultural land on the suburban fringe for £2,000 an acre and, after being refused permission for development, make a compensation claim which will be assessed as if it was "development land" worth ten times as much. The Irish Planning Institute, among many others, said this was inequitable because it requires the community at large - as in the case of Grange Developments - to "guarantee speculative profits to landowners". In his amendments to the Government's Planning Compensation Bill, the Minister for the Environment, proposed an important revision to the arbitration rules to deal with these distortions in land valuation. The effect of this move would be to ensure that compensation may not exceed the difference between the realistic market value of land immediately before a refusal of planning permission and its value after such a refusal. And it was a real indication that Mr Flynn was at last getting to the heart of the matter that the amendment was greeted with squeals of protest from the major housing developers (See Appendix 6).

It was due to widespread concern about the staggering increase in land prices during the late 1960s that the first Committee on the Price of Building Land was set up in 1971, under Mr Justice John Kenny. In the previous eight years, the average price for serviced land (having water supplies, sewerage and drainage) in Co Dublin went up by 530 per cent, as against an increase of just 64 per cent in the Consumer Price Index over the same period. To deal with this, the Kenny Report recommended a "designated area scheme" whereby land required for urban development would be designated by law and the local authority would be given power to acquire it at its existing use value, plus 25 per cent. However, nothing was done to implement the report because of the argument - untested in the courts - that it would be unconstitutional. The fact that Judge Kenny was a leading member of the High Court, with an expertise in constitutional law, appeared to count for nothing.

Following the failure of successive governments to act on the report, a Joint Oireachtas Committee on Building Land was set up in 1983. Two years later, it recommended a significant reform of the compulsory purchase rules, under which the value of land is arbitrated, to deal with this particular problem. Instead of allowing property owners full development value, the committee proposed that prevailing market conditions at any given time must be taken into account. "Any individual parcel of urban land might be used for an office development; all parcels together could not because there would simply be no demand for that quantity of office space", said the report. The committee also proposed a series of measures to remove distortions in the land market, more appropriate capital gains taxes and the withdrawal of State subsidies and other incentives from development on land not zoned for development. After four years lying on the shelf, the Joint Oireachtas Committee's report has been taken on board, at least in part, by Padraig Flynn through his proposed change in the valuation rules. Thus, there is some chance that land acquisition - together with the allied issue of compensation - won't in future prove such a problem for the local authorities as it has in the past.

In the notorious XJS case, Dun Laoghaire Corporation was put to the pin of its collar resisting a massive compensation claim from a company controlled by garage proprietors Murphy and Gunn. They had bought 24 acres of scrubland on Rocheshill, in Killiney, from the Malahide Estate for just £40,000 - a price which reflected the fact that it had no real development potential. But shortly after being refused planning permission for a housing scheme on the site, in a poorly-worded Bord Pleanala decision signed by Anthony Lambert, Ray Burke's constituency advisor, XJS Investments lodged a compensation claim for over £2 million. With strong backing - including professional expertise - from local associations and community groups, Dun Laoghaire Corporation fought the claim, demonstrating that the characteristics of the site meant that it could not be developed except at enormous expense. The arbitration hearing lasted a week and, in the end, XJS was awarded £150,000 in compensation - less than ten per cent of what it had so confidently sought, but still a tidy sum on a £40,000 investment. Not long afterwards, in a private deal, the Corporation bought 21 acres of Rocheshill from XJS for an additional £70,000 and it will now be conserved in perpetuity as public open space. Killiney Golf Club simultaneously purchased the remaining three acres adjoining its golf course from XJS for a reputed £24,000. In total, including costs, Irish taxpayers have had to pay at least a quarter of a million pounds to protect Rocheshill - something the legislation patently failed to do.

One of the issues which the Rocheshill and Grange cases had in common was the failure of Bord Pleanala to cite "non-compensatable" reasons for refusing permission - such as the non-availability of services or the danger of creating a traffic hazard. In the interests of protecting local authorities against compensation claims, the appeals board has now been directed to specify such reasons, where these apply, using the precise formula of words contained in Section 56 of the 1963 Planning Act. But the law should also be amended to give local authorities the option to purchase land which is the subject of a compensation claim. At present, such an option does not exist and, even after a successfully pursuing a claim for compensation, as in the Grange case, the land would remain in private hands and its owner would be entitled to come back in 14 years with a fresh planning application. (Under Mr Flynn's amendments, the local authorities would have an open-ended right to recover money paid out in compensation in the event of land being developed).

All in all, it is hard to imagine that this is what Eamon de Valera envisaged when he drafted the Irish Constitution. As Nuala O Faolain wrote in *The Irish Times:* "Perhaps this is because he was so honest. He was a man of such absolute personal austerity that perhaps he couldn't imagine that a great many Irish people would happily put their own private enrichment before the interests of the country. He obviously hoped for consensus on the goal of 'frugal comfort'. He was talking, of course, about frugal comfort for all - the all was what mattered. He plainly didn't envisage lavish comfort for some, and penury for the many. He could never have anticipated the tangled saga of planning permissions, auctioneers, contractors, suppliers and other beneficiaries of big builders, friendships, political alliances, scratching of backs, nods, winks and general skulduggery which are inseparable, in the common mind, from the very notion of developable land... Mr de Valera can never have meant the taxpayers of Ireland to have to hand over £2 million to Grange Developments who, in effect, are Mr Brennan and Mr McGowan to 'compensate' them for the supposed profit they would have made had they been allowed to build houses on land which they happen to own".

Father Paul Freeney, an outspoken Catholic priest who served in the developing dormitory town of Leixlip, Co. Kildare, took a jaundiced view of property speculators and their activities. Writing in the December 1971 issue of *Plan* magazine, he railed against the "faceless men" with chequebooks who were buying up land for housing in the Leixlip area. "The houses are sold with airy assurances that they are convenient to church, schools, shops, playing fields etc. Rubbish! No reference to the fact that the church is a little village church, that the school is a tiny village school, or that the same speculators have their mouths watering and their chequebooks waving to get at the local GAA field. No reference to the fact that it is the people of Leixlip, old and new, who will have to foot the bill for new schools, churches and community facilities, with not a brass penny from the speculators towards the facilities they so glibly and cynically boast of".

Fifteen years later, in a speech at the Dublin Crisis Conference, Father

Freeney appealed to the authorities to adopt a more humane approach to planning. "When the statistics, the economics and the grandiose schemes are plotted, it should not be too much to ask that the social dimension be considered, the real human conditions. People are not just bricks, mortar and concrete", he declared. "I hope that we will listen to those who live in the new suburbs and their opinions will be respected - not because they are clever or professional, but because they are the people who must live in these little boxes we call houses. If they are to form vigorous communities, they must not feel that those who designed their homes and their environment have no interest in whether they can live there happily. We cannot expect to plan away loneliness or stress or frutration, but there must be no need to adopt plans that can hardly produce anything else".

The planners are facing other challenges, too. In February 1989, at a debate on the future of Dublin organised by the Irish Planning Institute, Uinseann MacEoin, the architect and conservationist, said they would need an "iron-clad resolve" to prevent development mushrooming alongside the western by-pass motorway. Already, plans are being laid for a mammoth "regional shopping centre", with 1.5 million square feet of retail space, on a site in Palmerstown adjoining the interchange between the western by-pass and the Lucan/Galway road. The staggering scale of this scheme maybe measured by the fact that the site covers 200 acres of land, of which 50 acres would be set aside as a car park for between 8,000 and 10,000 cars. Modelled on the equally gargantuan Metrocentre on Tyneside, in the northeast of England, it is the brainchild of Tom Gilmartin, an Irish-born property developer who has been based in London for many years. Mr Gilmartin, who maintains the lowest of profiles, was involved in "assembling" the Bachelors Walk site in the city for the shopping centre planned by Arlington Securities. He also managed to persuade Padraig Flynn to extend the boundary of the Liffey Quays urban renewal designated area northwards to Abbey Street so that it would become more lucrative to acquire and redevelop the property there, too.

However, it was not long before Mr Gilmartin switched his attention to Palmerstown. Living in England, he was among the first to grasp the significance of the western by-pass as a vehicle for development, just like the M25 around London. This new "orbital motorway" opened up a whole range of opportunities for warehousing, industrial estates, "business parks", out-of-town offices - and shopping centres. The problem for Mr Gilmartin is that there is no provision in the Dublin County Development Plan for a huge retail facility in Palmerstown - not least because it would undermine the viability of the smaller "town centre" schemes planned for Tallaght, Lucan/Clondalkin and Blanchardstown. And because of its enormous scale, a "regional shopping centre" in Palmerstown would serve as a counter-magnet to the city centre, undermining its traditional role as the main shopping area in the State. Dublin Corporation, in the draft City Development Plan, identifies it as "the single most important objective in land use planning terms to reinforce the core of Dublin as the commercial, cultural and social centre of the metropolitan area". Ironically, however, it was the Corporation which provided Tom Gilmartin with the largest single chunk of his Palmerstown site, by selling him 70 acres of land in May 1989, for £5 million. So much for official platitudes about "reinforcing the core of Dublin".

But then, there has always been a strong element of *laissez faire* about planning in Dublin. Thus, when the Green Property Company sought permission in 1987 to double the size of the "town centre" it was planning for Blanchardstown, from 350,000 to three-quarters of a million square feet, the then county manager, George Redmond, saw no reason to refuse. "These fellows have done their sums and this is what they believe will work. Who are we to say it won't?, he declared. When it was put to him that this was a *laissez faire* argument which seemed to dispense with the need for any planning at all, Mr. Redmond said planners could not ignore market forces. And when the City Centre Business Association appealed against it, on the grounds that such a gargantuan shopping centre in Blanchardstown would take business away from the core of Dublin, Bord Pleanala - acting on the recommendation of Liam Tobin, the board's senior planning inspector - rejected their case and gave the green light to Green Property. Tom Gillmartin's Palmerstown scheme involves driving an even larger coach-and-four through the County Development Plan, but with powerful political support - not least from the Minister for the Environment, Padraig Flynn - who's to say that "market forces" won't prevail here, too?

4

Stopping the Rot

All over Europe, people are moving back to the centre of cities. It's happening not just in Paris and Florence, but in Belfast and Glasgow, too. It's even happening in Cork and Galway and, very slowly and spontaneously, with little or no encouragement from the powers-that-be, it's starting to happen in Dublin - at last. Fifteen years ago, Deirdre Kelly's Living City Group was almost alone in calling for the centre of Dublin to be maintained and developed as "the living heart of a capital city". Now, across the entire spectrum - including the Society of Chartered Surveyors, which represents many of those at the coal-face of the property world - people are looking at the potential of the inner city as a place to live.

One of the catalysts, ironically, was ERDO's controversial strategy for the Dublin region and, in particular, its dismissive conclusion that there was "not a good case under present circumstances" for locating even an extra 10,000 people - a tiny fraction of the total expected population increase - in the inner city area. What the ERDO strategists neglected to take into account was that families with three or four children are no longer "standard" these days. A large and growing proportion of the housing market is made up of young single people, separated people whose marriages have broken down and older couples with their children reared. And some of them are clearly seeking an alternative to what the chartered surveyors called the "monotony, social segregation, repetitive architecture, child-orientation and daily commuting" associated with the suburbs.

As things stand, however, there is no real encouragement for people to buy houses in the inner city; indeed, the highly-discriminatory structure of State housing subsidies - which serves little social purpose other than to keep private house-building firms in business - actively discourages such a move by first-time house-buyers, denying them a free choice. Thus, the £2,000 grant is available only for the purchase of new houses; anyone buying a second-hand house, in the inner city or elsewhere, not only forfeits the grant but they also have to pay stamp duty, at the average rate of four per cent on houses costing between £20,000 and £50,000. For young first-time buyers counting every penny, this double penalty is too great. "On a cheap house costing £30,000 at the far end of Clonsilla, versus an artisan house selling for the same price off the North Circular Road, the difference would work out at £3,200", says Liam O'Donnell, president of the Institute of Professional Auctioneers and Valuers. "On top of that, they might have to pay out £500 in legal fees for a search on the title, plus £200 for a building society surveyor's report, and all of this tilts the balance in favour of the outer suburban house and against the inner city one".

As a result, young married couples are almost forced into what could become a life-time of commuting from the far-distant suburbs when they might have settled for a house in the city. The consequences for Dublin as a whole are equally disastrous because the much-needed "new blood" which could help to revitalise older, twilight areas of the city is being diverted to greenfield sites on the periphery, swallowing up valuable agriculural land. And what's left behind is a declining, ageing population increasingly incapable of sustaining the range of social facilities which once existed in the heart of Dublin, let alone maintain its housing stock. This has been dramatically illustrated over the past 20 years by the relentless closure of inner city schools, churches, hospitals and even corner shops as well as the alarming spread of dereliction throughout the area. Over the same period, we have seen an explosion of similar facilities in the outer suburbs to cater for the needs of families who have moved out from the city. Even Sean Cromien, Secretary of the Department of Finance, admitted recently that this represented a "waste" of scarce public resources - a view shared by an increasing number of economists and planners.

But over the past 30 years or more, the combined forces of public and private investment, together with the planning process itself, have been mobilised in a single direction - towards abandoning the city to offices and roads in favour of a policy of building up the suburbs. Even Dublin Corporation's much-praised inner city schemes represent a relative fraction of that authority's housing output over the past fifteen years. And when it comes to industrial investment (excluding the I.D.A.), only three per cent of new factory space built in the Dublin area since 1962 has been located in the inner city. But now, we've actually reached the stage where even the relatively new suburban schools are beginning to close down because there are no longer enough children to keep them going. In Kilbarrack, which was developed in the early 1970s, one of the two 24-classroom primary schools will close this year because the number of pupils there has fallen from a peak of 900 to just 330. In Bonnybrook, also on the northside, the boys and girls national schools amalgamated for the same reason in 1988, and a similar fate lies in store for dozens of other parishes where children of the same age group all grew up together.

At the same time, according to a survey carried out by Corporation planners in 1985, the inner city area is littered with large and small derelict sites with an aggregate area of 160 acres - more than six times the size of St Stephen's Green - and this figure does not include all of the redundant dockland area as well as a considerable amount of under-utilised land (e.g. Grangegorman and the various Army barracks). Neither does it include the alarming number of buildings in the city centre which lie empty, apart from shops at street-level, because the owners are reluctant to let their upper floors for residential use. Though the Rent Restrictions Act went out in 1982, many of them still believe they would not get a fair return. Tenants might also have to be compensated, or even rehoused, in the case of redevelopment, so it makes more sense to retain property in commercial "use", even though the upper floors are not used at all. Yet, as the Corporation's planners warn, when premises are left vacant, there is a steady deterioration of the fabric, leading to the eventual loss of the building through neglect.

Much of the 11 million square feet of modern office space built in the city since 1960 has been concentrated in and around the southside Georgian core, where "urban renewal" was least required, leaving the northside and other less-favoured areas more run-down than ever. In a discussion document on the inner city prepared by the Corporation's planning department, there is an explicit recognition that the policy of trying to attract office development into areas outside the prime office zone has been a failure, and the planners are now proposing that these areas should be rezoned for residential use. Yet many property owners in marginal areas like the north inner city are still suffering from what might be termed a "lepreachaun-with-a-crock-of-gold mentality", believing - wrongly, in most cases - that they're sitting on potential office sites and that it's only a matter of time until some developer with a big chequebook arrives on the scene. Indeed, this entirely misplaced expectation of hitting the speculative jackpot has become one of the main barriers to realistic urban renewal by making it nearly impossible to acquire land in the inner city at a price which would make residential development economically viable.

Three years ago, the Society of Chartered Surveyors concluded that housing offers "the greatest potential" for inner city renewal. But until recently, property developers have shown little inclination to build private flats or houses in the inner city; indeed, apart from flats built in association with new office developments, hardly any private housing has been provided within the canal ring over the past 25 years. And the reason is simple - because the developers did not perceive that there was any real demand for inner city housing. "If the market isn't there, one cannot expect entrepreneurs to take what would be regarded as high risks in an area which has an unacceptable physical and social environment", says Michael Greene, director of the Construction Industry Federation.

The inner city is seen as physically unacceptable because of all the dereliction and decay, and socially unacceptable because of crime, vandalism and the fact that local authority housing accounts for almost 40 per cent of the existing stock - the highest proportion in the Republic. "No matter where you are in the inner city, you're not going to be very far from Corporation housing", said one seasoned observer, "and the same goes for derelict sites". It's no wonder, then, that property developers have given the inner city a wide berth, preferring to sink their money in "safe" areas like Ballsbridge, Clontarf and Donnybrook or, indeed, almost anywhere along the "Gold Coast" around Dublin Bay.

In recent years, the planners have intervened to insist on the provision of a "residential content" in most large commercial developments, and permission for such schemes is usually conditional on the inclusion of a number of apartments. Quite often, however, these turn out to be "phantom flats" which are never actually let. In 1983, for example, Power Securities obtained permission for an office development in the back gardens of four Georgian houses on St Stephen's Green on condition that one of these houses would be converted into three flats and another would be retained in residential use. Even before the scheme was finished, it was "sold on" to Canada Life but, six years later, the "residential content" remains unoccupied. It exists only on paper.

The big insurance companies and pension funds, who own much of the property in the city centre, have a horror of "mixed use" buildings of any kind, and this reflects the prejudices of their commercial tenants. "Those who occupy offices or shops seek a certain self-containment", one leading chartered surveyor said. "They don't want people in flats overhead who would have access to the building after six o'clock in the evening. So what you would have to do is provide a separate staircase and lift, as well as complete fire separation, and all of this costs money". Another surveyor advanced the rather paranoid view that one of the upper-floor flats might be "turned into a brothel", devaluing the entire property. It is also true, however, that the financial institutions simply prefer commercial use because it doesn't involve the same "hassle" as dealing with people. It also yields much higher rents.

Pension fund managers must always seek to maximise their returns so that they will be in a position to meet long-term commitments to policy-holders, and their power in the property market is such that they virtually have a stranglehold on investment decisions. Thus, developers who want to "sell on" a new building to one of the big institutional investors - as most of them do - have to produce the kind of "package" that they would be prepared to purchase. And since the developers would generally make a larger profit on such a deal rather than, say, by selling on to an owner occupier, the tendency to comply with what the pension fund managers want is almost overwhelming. This was illustrated by the row over Harcourt Terrace, where the Regency centrepiece, with its imposing portico, had become an eyesore after years of neglect in the hands of the Legion of Mary. Developers Oliver Caffrey and Peter Ledbetter bought the place in 1987 and made plans to demolish the building, retaining only the front facade in a scheme designed by Burke Kennedy, Doyle and Partners. They actually admitted at Bord Pleanala hearing in August 1988 that it would be technically possible and even cheaper to refurbish the existing building, and the main reason why this wasn't being done was that the end-product would not be worth as much as a purpose-built office block - at least in the eyes of a pension fund manager.

The unsympathetic attitude to the inner city among banks, building societies

The former Molly Bloom's pub on the corner of Arran Quay and Queen Street, which has been butchered by Bargaintown Ltd to provide an extension to its furniture showrooms. (Photograph by Pat Langan).

The pedimented centrepiece of Sarsfield Quay, the only quay along the Liffey which was designed as a unified composition, in 1985 (above) and (below) the same quay four years later after the buildings were needlessly demolished by Dublin Corporation. (Photographs by The Irish Times and Pat Langan).

and insurance companies is also a serious stumbling block. According to Senator David Norris, chairman of the North Great George's Street Preservation Society, a "blacklist" - official or unofficial - has been in operation with regard to specific areas of the city, such as Dublin 1. "It is possible to get a mortgage, bridging finance and insurance, but it's bloody difficult", he said. "And one of the most aggravating things about it is that you could pay out money for a building society surveyor's report, thinking that you had a chance, only to discover that you were going to be turned down automatically on the basis of geographical location". This is not due purely to prejudice. It also reflects the fact that, especially on the northside, the combined cost of buying and refurbishing a run-down house can often greatly exceed its re-sale value.

The building societies also seem reluctant to give mortgages to people buying flats in converted Georgian houses - mainly because they take a rather jaundiced view of old buildings anyway. But then, they have always been behind the times; not too long ago, before purpose-built apartments became commonplace, they wouldn't advance money on them either. Indeed, at one stage, the building societies interpreted their role so narrowly that it was difficult to get a mortgage for a secondhand house, in the inner city or anywhere else. These antediluvian attitudes will have to change if Georgian Dublin is to be saved. Most 18th century houses are too large to be restored by individuals or to be lived in as single-family dwellings. One solution to this problem would be to encourage - or force - the banks and building societies to provide mortgages for "condominium" developments or "flying freeholds", i.e. the conversion of large houses into floor-by-floor flats. If such loans were available, according to property experts, it would be possible to buy and refurbish an 800 sq. ft, flat for around £35,000 - a price which could be afforded by many.

Senator Norris was not alone in drawing attention to another major deficiency - the fact that the urban renewal tax incentives, as originally cast, were heavily biased against people who want to renovate a house to live in. "They only worked for commercial investors", he says. "So if you were gutting a listed Georgian house to turn it into offices or flats, the Government rewarded you with a bucketful of tax breaks. But if you just wanted to preserve it as a house, thereby helping to keep the city alive and save its architectural heritage, they gave you absolutely nothing". Thus, business firms renting space in a Georgian house from a PAYE taxpayer are able to avail of generous tax concessions while the unfortunate PAYE person, who restored the house in the first place, received no encouragement whatever. Senator Norris pressed the Government to provide an incentive to such hard-pressed preservationists by allowing them to set off their expenses in carrying out this work against their PAYE tax liability - and, to his delight, the Minister for Finance, Albert Reynolds, agreed to do so. As a result, anyone who restores for owner-occupation an architecturally-important building in the urban renewal areas throughout the country be entitled to write off 50 per cent of their outlay against their taxable income, spread over five years. It has been left to the Commissioners of Public Works to determine which buildings will qualify as being of "significant scientific, historical, architectural or aesthetic interest", and they may interpret this generously or restrictively, but the Minister's concession amounts to the single most important gesture towards architectural conservation by any Irish Government.

What it does, in effect, is to transform listed buildings from liabilities into assets, making it realistic as well as desirable to preserve the city's architectural heritage - instead of viewing this as an intolerable burden. And the estimated annual cost to the Exchequer, at £1 million in lost revenue, is more than justified. After all, is the community which by listing buildings for preservation is saying that it wants those buildings to be preserved. Thus, there was always an onus on the Government to provide special grants or tax incentives for the maintenance and refurbishment of buildings which are deemed to be of architectural or historic interest. In European Architectural Heritage Year (1975), the Government signed the Declaration of Amsterdam guaranteeing full support for the preservation of Ireland's architectural heritage as part of the common heritage of Europe. Ten years later, Dr Maurice Craig, the distinguished architectural historian, could say that our legislation and funding provision in this area "is so farcically inadequate as to be virtually non-existent. In this respect, we are at the bottom of the European league". Indeed, according to An Taisce estimates, of the mainly Georgian buildings listed for preservation (List 1) in the 1980 City Development Plan, at least 50 have been subjected to material alteration over the past seven or eight years. And of those scheduled for "protection" (List 2), up to 80 have already been demolished or planning permission has been granted for their demolition.

The ludicrous inadequacy of the listing system was dramatically underlined in 1988 by the cases of Clare Street and Eccles Street. One of the finest mid-

18th century houses in Dublin, No. 29 Clare Street was acquired in the early 1970s by the Wexford-born businessman Jim Stafford, then heavily involved in property development and now a leading light in Century Communications. He sought planning permission to demolish the building, along with another next door, to make way for an office development but, by the time this came through, the property market had collapsed and there was little point in proceeding. Meanwhile, No. 29 was left vacant and its condition steadily deteriorated. The lead was removed, probably stolen, from the valley gutters and the house suffered severe water penetration which, in turn, produced outbreaks of wet and dry rot. Davis King, the adjoining owners, took legal action against Mespil Ltd, Stafford's "offshore" company, to compel him to carry out repairs, but the condition of the house was now so poor that the Corporation's dangerous buildings section ordered the removal of the top two floors. However, since the house was listed for protection, the planners insisted that the remaining floors be roofed temporarily to protect the magnificent staircase hall, in particular. In February 1989, the liquidator of Mr Stafford's company sold the property for £718,000 to Roy Strudwick's Ryde International, the British developers who had earlier bought the Irish Sweeps site in Ballsbridge for £6.5 million.

In Eccles Street, it was the Mater Hospital - rather than some property speculator - which was to blame. The Mater, which is run by the Sisters of Mercy, had already demolished the north side of the street to clear the way for a new private hospital and a vast area of surface car parking. And the casualties of this scorched earth policy included the terrace of Georgian houses occupied for many year by the Dominican Convent as well as the house - No. 7 - which served as a home, at least in James Joyce's imagination, for Leopold and Molly Bloom. But the Mater did not confine itself to its own side of Eccles Street. For many years, the hospital had been buying up property on the other side, too, presumably to provide more *lebensraum* for its ever-expanding activities. However, instead of making good use of this property, the hospital illegally blocked up the doorways and windows of three listed houses and left several others ominously vacant. In December 1987 the Dublin City Association of An Taisce wrote to the Mater's chief executive, Gearoid MacGabhann, seeking a meeting to discuss what plans, if any, the hospital had in mind for the south side of the street. But the only response the association received was a letter from chartered surveyors Harrington Bannon saying that they were "not in a position" to disclose any information about their client's properties and they didn't feel that a meeting would "serve any useful purpose"

Things came to a head in February 1988 when the Mater invited the Corporation's dangerous buildings section to inspect three vacant mid-terrace Georgian houses near the corner of Nelson Street. The inspection was carried out by a Mr Harris, who concluded that all three houses were in a "dangerous" condition and demolition to a safe level would be necessary. Within days the hospital received three orders rubber-stamped with the name C.P. Dardis, the Corporation's civic and amenities architect, requiring the houses to be demolished to first or second-floor cill levels, and a demolition crew moved in just one week later. On the same day, however, the houses were occupied by Students Against the Destruction of Dublin, who hung out huge banners bearing such logans as "Mercy Nuns Prey Not" and "We Uphold Bloom". The very next day, the Mater obtained a High Court injunction against the students and they agreed to withdraw, allowing demolition work to resume - but not before moving to obtain a counter injunction against the hospital on the grounds that it should not be demolishing listed buildings without planning permission. And while this action was unsuccessful, it did serve a very useful purpose in flushing out the full extent of the Mater's property holding on the south side of the street. Indeed, it transpired that the hospital - which received £24.5 million from the State in 1988 - had bought up to twenty-eight of the forty-two houses involved, as well as three more in Nelson Street, with the aid of funds raised from the M.H. (Mater Hospital) Pools. Of the total, two are totally derelict, 13 are either vacant or substantially vacant - included the three condemned by the Corporation - and at least two more, at the corner of Nelson Street, were threatened with demolition. As Ian Lumley, of An Taisce, commented in relation to the M.H. Pools, "It is shocking to think of the number of Dublin people who thought they were subscribing to a worthy charity when, in fact, they were contributing to the destruction of their own city".

From the affidavit sworn by Mr MacGabhann for the High Court case, it emerged that the Mater had realised in May 1986 that the roofs of the houses were in need of major repair, but no work was carried out. A year later, a report by the hospital's consulting engineers pointed to the inevitable consequences of this lack of maintenance, referring to "continuous water penetration which considerably weakened the roof structure, top floor and second floor". By January 1988, not surprisingly, another inspection by the consulting engineers found that "further substantial deterioration" had occurred to such a degree that the roofs and floors had become "structurally unsound". It was at this point that the Mater invited the Corporation's dangerous buildings section to inspect the three houses - again, with inevitable consequences. And though a local firm of architects, Breen Kelly, who had restored a Georgian house on the street, argued that it would have been a "perfectly practical" proposition to renovate rather than demolish the Mater's three houses, it was the opinion of the dangerous buildings section which prevailed - even though none of the eight area inspectors were qualified architects or structural engineers. Indeed, a 1967 Supreme Court judgement declared that, in the case of appeals to the District Court against dangerous buildings orders, a court may "in no way alter or modify the works directed to be carried out, or the conditions under which they are to be carried out, or review the opinion of the sanitary authority as to the appropriateness of the works required to be carried out or enter into the question of whether the structure is or is not a dangerous structure"

In the Eccles Street case, the Corporation's planners were not even informed in advance that dangerous buildings orders were being issued in respect of houses which had been listed for protection in the City Development Plan. Yet, over the previous two years, they had written a series of letter to the Mater Hospital seeking assurances that the houses it owned on the south side of the street would be maintained. Now, the planners - and the City Council's planning committee - have laid down a firm marker against further demolitions on Eccles Street by upgrading many of the surviving houses from List 2 to List 1. The major problem they face, however, is that there is in fact no statutory basis under the Planning Acts for the listing of buildings; indeed, the procedure is entirely *ad hoc* because it is not mentioned anywhere in the legislation. The 1963 Planning Act is remarkably silent on architectural conservation, other than in the vague context of preserving "amenities". It lays down no nationally-consistent system for listing buildings, nor is it mandatory on the planning authorities to dray up any list and there is also no provision for the designation of conservation areas, where special controls might apply. Thus, the first priority must be to give listed buildings and conservation areas proper status in law, with additional legal powers given to the local authorities to deal with the problem of creeping dereliction by carrying out repairs when deliberate neglect arises - registering the cost as a charge against the property. However, when Michael Keating TD (PD) asked the Minister for the Environ-

St. Georges Church, in Hardwicke Place, Dublin's most important classical church, which is facing closure like many other inner city Protestant churches. (Photograph: The Irish Times).

ment, Padraig Flynn, in February 1988 if he had any plans to strengthen the flimsy legislative protection for listed buildings, the Minister suggested that the existing powers were adequate and he had "no proposals at present" to change the situation. End of story.

The case of Drogheda Grammar School should give Mr. Flynn pause for thought. This was a group of mid-18th century buildings in Laurence Street, Drogheda, which had fallen into the hands of local property speculators in 1978. Within two years, they had applied for planning permission to demolish the former Dr Clarke's Free School and the Singleton House, both dating from around 1740, the later in its day probably the finest Georgian town house outside Dublin. But as the fabric of the buildings was allowed to deteriorate, the local preservation society obtained a High Court injunction in 1980 restraining unauthorised demolition. And though Drogheda Corporation granted permission to the speculators, trading as DGS Ltd, to demolish the buildings, this decision was successfully appealed to Bord Pleanala, which insisted that they must be preserved. In 1986, after years of neglect had taken its toll, DGS again sought permission to demolish the former grammer school and build town houses on the site. But the Corporation's decision, confirmed on appeal by Bord Pleanala in 1987, required the facades to be retained. Almost two years later, with the site still undeveloped, the Corporation made the mistake of issuing a dangerous buildings notice to DGS Ltd, requiring certain remedial works to be carried out and, thus armed, the speculators brought in a demolition crew at four o'clock one Sunday morning in July 1989 and had the grammar school pulled down. The gardai were called, but said they could do nothing. Belatedly, two Corporation officials turned up on the site while the illegal work was in progress but, instead of ordering demolition to cease forthwith, they actually sanctioned its continuation to a "safe level", which was interpreted as meaning that even the ground-floor facade could be swept away. It was left to Edward O'Doherty, vice-president of the Louth Archaeological Society and Fergus O'Dowd, a Fine Gael alderman, to uphold the law by going to the High Court for a mandatory order against DGS Ltd. And what an order it was. Granted by Mr. Justice Lardner on July 31st., 1989, it required the speculators - at their own expense - to erect a palisade fence around the entire site within five days. They were also required to hire a contractor to salvage the rubble on the site and then weatherproof it, as well as the surviving vaulted basements, under the direction of the preservation society's architect,

John Redmill. The directors of DGS Ltd also faced the prospect of being cited for contempt, and possibly even imprisoned, over the company's defiance of the 1980 High Court injunction. Either way, the outcome of the Drogheda Grammar School case could prove a powerful deterrent for others contemplating weekend demolition jobs on Ireland's architectural heritage.

There are also lessons on how not to restore historic buildings. In March 1988, as a gesture to the Dublin Millennium, the Electricity Supply Board announced that it was going to restore a terrace of eight Georgian houses on Upper Mount Street as well as two on Lower Fitzwilliam Street, linking them all together at the rear with catwalks in a glass-roofed atrium. The scheme, costed at £4 million, was seen by conservationists as an attempt by the ESB to atone for the destruction of 16 Georgian houses in Lower Fitzwilliam Street on the site of its main headquarters office building. Just one year later, while the "restoration" was in progress, a large chunk of two of the Upper Mount Street houses collapsed into the street and they had to be demolished. The houses involved had never been the best to begin with and were made even worse over the years by the ESB's insertion of linking corridors to make them more serviceable as office. But instead of carrying out a minimalist restoration, working with the existing fabric, the ESB embarked on what was, in effect, a radical reconstruction, gutting so much of the interiors that there was precious little left to hold the buildings together. Even the key house at the corner of Merrion Square was so destabilised by the renovations that the top floors had to be taken down. There was some irony in the fact that the architect involved was Sam Stephenson, at one time Dublin's most controversial designer, and that the contractors were John Paul, who had built his Civic Offices at Wood Quay. The debacle in Upper Mount Street was all the more ironic given the ebullient Mr Stephenson's Pauline conversion, revealed to a Law Society seminar in February, 1988. "I used to be an apostle of modern architecture, but I've given up that religion completely and I'm now an aetheist", he declared. "I go to bed with Palladio in the evening and get up with Lutyens". Be that as it may - and there can be no doubt that Sam has mellowed over the years - he and his clients, the ESB, should have followed Ian Lumley's example in Henrietta Street in pulling an old Georgian house back together again through minimal intervention. It also costs a lot less.

The same lesson might have been learned by the Royal College of Surgeons, in relation to Mercer's Hospital. In 1984, when the college acquired the hospital, there was considerable relief in conservation circles that it hadn't fallen into the hands of rapacious speculators. The grounds for optimism were underlined by an imaginative renovation of the late 1950s nurses home to provide student accommodation. Before long, however, it became clear that the college's plans for the main hospital buildings were much less sensitive. The oldest building in the group was the original charitable infirmary founded by Mary Mercer in 1740; indeed, part of the proceeds of the world premiere of Handel's Messiah in the old Fishamble Street music hall helped to build it. On one side, there was a crude barracks-style extension and on the other, facing South King Street, an elaborate Victorian edifice (c. 1888) which closes the vista from St. Stephen's Green. But instead of working within the fabric of the best of these buildings, the college sought to make them fit new uses for which they were entirely unsuited - notably, a huge open-plan library. Talks with An Taisce got nowhere and it took the intervention of David Slattery, the architect responsible for the Custom House restoration, who is now Ireland's leading expert on stone, to save the granite facade of the mid-18th century building. The earlier advice from the college's architects, Brian O'Halloran and Associates, and consulting engineer, Joe McCullough, at one time a leading light in An Taisce, was the this would create more problems than it was worth. The college was also confronted by the usual unsympathetic approach of Dublin Corporation's fire officers, who seem to believe that no historic building can be adapted safely to new uses without being ripped apart. And that is essentially what happened to Mercer's ; except for the main facades, the hospital was demolished. Meanwhile, the College of Surgeons was left with a large car park site directly adjoining its main buildings which would have been eminently suitable for the erection of a library. But now, as a result of its own misconceived plans, this site looks as if it will lie fallow for the forseeable future while Mary Mercer's legacy to the city is needlessly butchered.

There was more than enough butchery at Dublin Castle, too. For years, apart from the showpiece State Apartments, much of the castle - the most historic and, arguably, the most important group of buildings in the capital - was abandoned in varying stages of decay. Then, in 1986, the Government announced a £20 million "restoration" plan for the castle, mainly to provide a functional EC conference centre in time for Ireland's presidency of the Community during the first half of 1990. In reality, of course, large parts of the castle were demolished - including the Chief Secretary's galleried library,

114

behind City Hall - and replaced by more or less successful replicas or by new buildings in the currently fashionable post-modern style. The most welcome part of the scheme was the removal of the 19th century top storey of the Bedford Tower block, restoring it to its Malton print days - though the heavy "portcullis" windows of the stone-faced addition to this block clash with the light steel railings of the new hump-backed bridge directly in front. There is a fake moat underneath this bridge, with the ground-floor facade of the La Touche Bank, which stood on Castle Street, re-erected as an arcade along one side of it. But, ironically, the most exciting element of the reconstruction of the castle lies underground - and this is not a reference to the pretentious "European Hall", half-buried at basement level, where the EC leaders will meet. It is, in fact, a cavernous chamber, criss-crossed with catwalks, in which one can see revealed for the first time in centuries the base of the Powder Tower, a short stretch of the castle's original moat, a piece of the old city wall and, of all things, a Viking embankment which is older than the castle itself. This, indeed, is the only public bonus from the demolition of blocks 8, 9 and 10 - which, while it was under way, made the castle an ideal location for a television drama set in wartime London. But at the end of the "restoration" scheme, large parts of Dublin Castle are as abandoned as they were before it started, including the early 18th century Treasury building in the Lower Yard, the Revenue building to the rear of the State Apartments and the Ship Street Barracks. Only when these are rescued from decrepitude will the State be able to say that the castle has been saved.

The consultants who carried out the EC-funded study - SKC, DKM and Reid McHugh - strongly argue the case for architectural conservation. "No discussion on Inner City revitalisation can be complete without mentioning the need for refurbishment of derelict buildings. Renovation work on buildings in the Inner City is reflected in an increase in the value of neighbouring properties. Thus, the marginal social benefits of improvement work exceed the private marginal cost and property owners are likely to invest less than the socially optimal amount. This would seem to us to justify the payment of subsidies to encourage renovation work in the Inner City. The consultants recognise that this would be outside the scope of the ERDF [European Regional Development Fund] except in some limited cases. Nevertheless, there may be a case for a redirection of Exchequer funds from existing housing supports to finance a scheme in this area". Particularly welcome, because it's so long overdue, is their recommendation in favour of the restoration of Henrietta Street, the oldest and most palatial of the city's Georgian streets, at an overall cost of £6 million - though it remains to be seen what the proposed "major tourism theme project" would mean, who would pay for it and how it would be managed.

Successive governments seem to believe that they can have urban renewal on the cheap - a few incentives here and there, but no real money, and especially not the kind of investment which would be required to turn the situation around. This is partly due to the parsimonious attitude of the Department of Finance, but it also reflects the fact that Ministers regard the city as a quarry for the construction industry. They want to see development, lots of activity on the ground, without any regard for the long-term impact on the surrounding community or, indeed, the fabric of the city. And since the incentives are heavily biased in favour of commercial rather than residential development, as well as new buildings over old, the effect is predictable: the city's architectural heritage suffers and there is no discernible benefit for local communities. The State's own input is minimal - a paltry sum of two million pounds for environmental works to improve the appearance of urban renewal areas all over the country and a relatively small annual commitment to the refurbishment of Dublin Corporation's inner city flats.

Yet no package of tax incentives could be expected to reverse the chronic decline of the north inner city. In its present run-down condition, few commercial developers are going to be tempted to invest because rental values are so low that there is no prospect of making an economic return. This is borne out by the severe difficulties which Dublin Corporation has experienced in disposing of its sites in the north inner city designated area; for the first couple of years after the tax incentives were introduced, there were no takers at all. So if the fortunes of the area are to be lifted, it will obviously require some direct investment by the State. This could follow Belfast's example by designating the north inner city as a "housing action area", backed up by a concerted renewal programme which would be sufficiently flexible to tackle decay on several fronts. As well as refurbishing the Corporation's flats, it would have to provide funds to carry out external repairs to terraces of mixed tenure, to develop new housing on derelict sites and to provide home improvement grants - specifically targeted at the area - to encourage people to repair the privately-owned housing stock. Another idea which might be considered is "homesteading" - it has worked well in Belfast - which would involve the authorities acquiring run-down houses and assigning them at a peppercorn rent to private individuals who agree to undertake their restoration. And whatever such a programme might cost, it would be a relatively small sum when set alongside the startling misallocation of resources on other housing programmes - notably the home improvements scheme. The eventual out-turn on this scatter-gun scheme is estimated at no less than £250 million, of which at least half went to people installing aluminium replacement windows - often quite needlessly. Indeed, it would have been enough to cover the cost of refurbishing Dublin Corporation's *entire stock* of 11,608 inner city flats.

The spin-offs from a properly-targeted urban renewal programme would be significant. In Glasgow, where a concerted effort has been under way for ten years, they have found that up to 400 jobs are created or maintained for every 1,000 new residents - because of the boost in demand for a whole range of services, from TV repair shops, to hairdressers and dry cleaners. Newcomers to Glasgow's derelict east end, a major focus of the city's renewal effort, were not the outsiders and "Yuppies" which some of the planners feared, but people with strong roots in the area, often the sons and daughters of families who had been cleared out to Ballymun-style housing estates in the suburbs. The British Government has invested over £150 million in the renaissance of Glasgow, but this has "levered" three times as much money from the private sector because investors can see for themselves that the city really is moving in the right direction. None of them would have put their money into Glasgow ten years ago, when it was lumped with Liverpool in the basket of hopeless cases. Only public funds, wisely spent, could have turned the situation around.

There are also major inconsistencies the Government's overall urban policy - if that's what it could be called. While on the one hand - as the Dublin Crisis Conference *Manifesto for the City* pointed out - the Government is seeking to encourage renewal in designated areas, on the other, it is "directly funding massive urban blight in the areas affected by Dublin Corporation's extensive road-widening schemes". Individual Government departments, notably the Department of Health, are pursuing spending programmes which will further erode the primacy of the inner city and, in the case of the hospitals, are leaving us with a stock of architecturally-important but vacant buildings. The hospitals already lost include Mercer's, Sir Patrick Dun's, Dr Steevens's, the Richmond, Jervis Street and old St Vincent's, on the Green. If present policies continue unchanged, longer-term casualties will include the Adelaide, the Meath and the children's hospitals in Harcourt Street and Temple Street. Obviously, there is a need to centralise highly-expensive acute general hospital facilities. However, with the increasing reliance on "community medicine", there is surely a case for keeping at least some of these buildings open as community hospitals - such as Baggot Street - for the benefit of inner city residents. In any case, no hospital should be closed until an alternative use for the building has been clearly determined.

"Over the past 20 years, the inner city has lost far too many schools, especially second-level schools", the *Manifesto for the City* said. "These losses include the Dominican College, in Eccles Street; the Holy Faith, Dominick Street; the High School, Harcourt Street; the Loreto, North Great George's Street; the Sacred Heart Convent, Lower Leeson Street; Alexandra College, Earlsfort Terrace; King's Hospital (the Bluecoat School) in Blackhall Place together with St Andrew's School and Wesley College, formerly located in St Stephen's Green. In most cases, these schools have found new homes in the suburbs, but their departure has left the city poorer, socially and education-ally". Thus, if the thrust of public policy is to increase the population of the inner city, every effort must be made to retain the schools which survive because they will be needed in the future.

"To stave off ERDO's projected decline of 100,000 in the population of the existing built-up area will require a more rational use of resources, with the emphasis on inner city renewal and the need to conserve the city's housing stock", the *Manifesto for the City* went on. "This would involve either the abolition of the present grants scheme for new houses as well as the stamp duties charged on second-hand houses or the payment of an equal grant (perhaps half of the present figure) to the purchasers of both new and second-hand houses, again with no stamp duty charged on the latter. Only then will young married couples be able to buy homes in the existing built-up area instead of being forced to go out to the suburban periphery. It should be emphasised that the changes proposed here would apply only to first-time house-purchasers; others buying second-hand houses or 'trading up' would still have to pay stamp duty".

Dublin is a relatively small city, not a great metropolis, so it's never going to reach the dizzy heights of London, where a converted Victorian broom closet opposite Harrods - measuring all of 11 feet by six - was sold a few years ago for £36,500 (sterling). However, there is a burgeoning interest here in city centre apartments among people who appreciate the values of real urban living and, if this is sustained, Dublin could be on the verge of regenerating itself. In 1988, for example, six flats in South Anne Street and another half-dozen in Duke Street, built as part of the Royal Hibernian Way development, were snapped up at prices ranging from £38,000 to £90,000. Indeed, over a period of just eight months, the value of one single-bedroom apartment - at 400 square feet, barely large enough to swing a cat - went up by £20,000, to a staggering £58,000.

However, people will only invest their money in an area which they believe is on the way up, not down. To overcome negative perceptions of the inner city on this score, the Society of Chartered Surveyors - in their landmark study of the area, published in 1986 - suggested that regeneration should proceed on the basis of a "cellular" approach. This would mean selecting a large enough block of derelict inner city property to create self-sufficient (and secure) residential neighbourhoods - new "living cells" which would then "infuse life into the areas around them". The quality and design of these schemes "needs not to be just good, but needs to set new standards", the surveyors said. Only then, they believe, could an inner city residential development hope to capture the imagination of the target market, which they see as mainly single people and double-income married couples without children - "Yuppies", for the want of a better word. The cellular approach is also endorsed by the EC study consultants, who say it would provide "a focus and oportunity for local communities to participate in the process of revitalisation".

There is an urgent need to find new uses for old buildings, but in this vital area of recycling the fire regulations - which were clearly drafted with new structures in mind - can present serious difficulties. And since there is no specific exemption for listed buildings, compliance with a fire officer's requirements could involve sacrificing many of the very features which made them worth listing in the first place. These considerations would also apply to the conversion for residential use of the acres of empty floorspace on the upper floors of buildings in the city centre. Such a move would give a new lease of life to secondary shopping streets like South Great George's Street, and some of the buildings there which would be suitable candidates for this treatment include the marvellous South City Markets, as well as the nearby Central Hotel and former Dockrell shop building, both of which are substantially vacant. Even for new buildings, there is a plethora of by-laws and planning standards to be met - such as site coverage, plot ratio, open space and off-street parking - which, if rigidly imposed, could undermine the viability of city centre apartment schemes.

As the controversy over Wood Quay demonstrated, Dublin also has a rich archaeological heritage and this, too, needs to be protected. What it gets, though, is little more than lip-service. The row over Wood Quay - and, in particular, the long delays in building the Civic Offices - ensured that anything to do with archaeology in Dublin would be guaranteed to send a shudder down the spine of Corporation officials and developers alike. To this day, unlike other cities like Galway and Waterford, Dublin hasn't got its own City Archaeologist who, if funds were made available, might arrange a rolling programme of "digs" on known sites of archaelogical interest - long in advance of any new development. As a result, according to the December 1988 issue of *Archaeology Ireland*, the Corporation is "riding roughshod over archaeo-logical opinion and the heritage of Dublin" in granting planning permission for office developments in High Street and Winetavern Street, without making any provision for the sites to be properly excavated. All that's done, indeed, is to make permission conditional on raft-type foundations so as not to disturb the archaeological strata. As a result, a golden opportunity to excavate these sites in this generation is being shamelessly squandered.

Some of Dublin's most important landmarks are churches, but they are also under serious threat. Many of these buildings are very significant, both historically and architecturally, and they also happen to be in the hands of the Church of Ireland, which has seen its congregation in the inner city area fall precipitately from 40,000 a century ago to just 1,000 today. Thus, it is unrealistic to expect the Church to maintain all of the buildings it still holds and, at the same time, the Commissioners of Public Works say they are debarred for constitutional reasons from contributing to the preservation of buildings used for religious worship. If the threatened churches are to survive, a way around this impasse must be found - either by grant-aiding restoration works on the fabric of these buildings or by finding suitable new uses for them. The casualties already include St Peter's, in Aungier Street, which was demolished in 1980 to make way for a long-delayed YMCA centre; St. Nicholas and St. Luke's, on the Coombe, which was destroyed by fire after years of abandonment; St. Mary's, in Mary Street, where Wolfe Tone was baptised and Arthur Guinness married, which was sold in 1988 for conversion

Henrietta Street, oldest and grandest of Dublin's Georgian streets, which has been proposed for restoration as a "major tourism theme project", though there's uncertainty about whether this will actually happen. (Photograph by Pat Langan).

into a 'decor store'; St. Jude's, in Inchicore, where it took a determined campaign by the local heritage group to save the spire from been sold for salvage; the Free Church, in Great Charles Street, which was closed in the same year and put on the market for £50,000; and St. George's, in Hardwicke Place, by far the finest church in Dublin, with its multi-tiered steeple now held up by scaffolding, which was offered for sale in March 1989.

Meanwhile rigorous restraint needs to be applied to the redevelopment of streets which are slipping into commercial use. The grim-walled canyon of Lower Mount Street is the classic example of conversion to a single use category (offices), with disastrous consequences for the life of the street. John Kelly, the former Fine Gael backbench TD who can always be relied upon to produce quotable quotes, summed it up when he said Lower Mount Street had become so lifeless that it resembled "the view from the inside of a coffin". If more city centre streets are not to die in the same way, there will have to be a quantitative limit to the level of high-value office uses - for example, by setting and holding to a minimum residential content not just for individual buildings, but for streets as well - to prevent key areas being overpowered by office developments.

Land values - or, rather, land "hope" values - lie at the root of much of the dereliction and unbalanced development in the inner city. One of the main reasons why 160 acres of land is lying fallow is that the city is suffering from what the experts call "development inertia", caused by the inflated hopes of landowners that they are sitting on potential office development sites, with the long-term prospect of massive capital gains. The reality, however, is that there is a limited market for offices in Dublin and this is largely confined to south-eastern sector of the city; therefore, to be holding out for a Ballsbridge office price in, say, the Liberties is entirely unrealistic.

As a way of overcoming this problem, each landowner might be obliged to make an annual return of the value of their land to be assessed under a land tax scheme, as proposed in the Dublin Crisis Conference *Manifesto for the City*. "Different percentage tax rates could be established for different uses and the rates could also vary according to location. Thus, in north central Dublin, it could be at the preferential rate of one per cent for offices and retail uses, with a zero rate for industrial and residential while, on the southside, offices would incur a more penal rate of seven per cent, with shops paying three per cent and industrial and residential again rated at zero. Such a regime would serve the dual purpose of encouraging urban renewal in the area it is most needed, as well as recapturing some of the 'betterment' in values for the community''.

In February 1989, the Government introduced a Derelict Sites Bill, which would impose an annual levy on derelict land - whether sites or buildings - based on a percentage of their market value. This will at least end the inbuilt incentive to hoard derelict land, by removing the present inequitable situation whereby owners who maintain their properties must often pay commercial rates while those who take the roof off their buildings pay nothing. It remains to be seen if the local authorities - including Dublin Corporation - will actually use their powers under the new legislation to serve repairs notices on property owners who allow their buildings to fall into decay. Meanwhile, returns from the annual levy might be used to fund a grants scheme for owners of listed buildings who wish to keep them in good repair. In default of payment, the derelict sites levy could be registered as a charge against the property and there should also be a provision in cases of long-term default whereby ownership would pass to the local authority after, say, 10 years.

Finally, something will have to be done about air and water pollution in the city. Though Ballyfermot has been the principal focus of attention when it comes to smog, the fact remains that some of the highest single smoke pollution readings in recent years have been taken in the inner city, at Cornmarket and Mountjoy Square. And until the smog levels are substantially reduced, not only will the city's air remain unhealthy and unpleasant in winter, but even the buildings recently cleaned for the Millennium will revert to their sooty-black state before the turn of the century. Predictably, the coal lobby has opposed the implementation of effective "clean air" measures, even to the extent of going to court, but the Government is under a legal obligation to ensure that the EC's air pollution directive is complied with by April 1993. The only way to fulfill this obligation would be to speed up the designation of smoke control areas, backed up by a properly-funded grants scheme aimed at persuading householders to change over to smokeless fuels, such as natural gas.

In the case of water pollution, there is particular concern about the continuing deterioration of water quality in Dublin Bay - a prime recreational area, especially for inner city residents who don't have cars to travel further afield. The inner bay is so polluted by partially-treated sewage effluent that bacteria levels up to eight times the EC maximum limit were recorded at the Bull Wall in August 1988 and even Dollymount Strand, an EC-designated beach, can be hit by the spillover effects. Dun Laoghaire's sewage outfall at the West Pier caused intermittent pollution at nearby Seapoint, and plans were approved in 1988 for a £12 million pipeline to carry it across the Bay to Dublin Corporation's sewage treatment plant at Ringsend. But while this will clean up Seapoint, it can only worsen the already serious situation in the inner bay. Everyone knows that the technology is available to solve this problem, but it would involve spending over £40 million to upgrade the Ringsend plant to full tertiary treatment. However, this project is not included in the Government's application for EC structural funds, apparently because it will have to await the completion of a long-promised water quality management plan for Dublin Bay.

SAVING THE CITY

Noise, too, should not be discounted as a form of pollution, especially in the built-up urban environment. Traffic is the major source of noise and, if the city is to become a more attractive place to live, traffic - and, therefore, noise - levels will have to be reduced. At present, there are no guidelines, let alone statutory provisions, on what noise levels would be "acceptable" for a residence beside a road. As a first step towards dealing with the problem, it would be essential to recognise and accept that the inner city is a place where people live - and sleep.

5

What is to be done?

What do we mean by the city? The question was one which exercised Lewis Mumford in the 1960s when, all around him, cities were being destroyed and rebuilt. "The city", he wrote, "is the form and symbol of an integrated social relationship; it is the seat of the temple, the market, the hall of justice and the academy of learning. It is also a conscious work of art, and it holds within its communal framework many simpler and more personal forms of art. Mind takes form in the city; and in turn, urban forms condition the mind. For space, no less than time, is artfully reorganised in cities; in boundary lines and silhouettes, in the fixing of horizontal planes and vertical peaks, in utilising or denying the natural site, the city records the attitude of a culture and an epoch to the fundamental facts of its existence. The dome and the spire, the open avenue and the closed court, tell the story not merely of different physical accommodations but of essentially different conceptions of man's destiny. The city is both a physical utility for collective living and a symbol of those collective purposes and unanimities that arise under such favouring circumstance. With language itself, it remains man's greatest work of art''.

The value of Dublin's historic core is fulsomely recognised by the consultants who carried out the EC study. "The physical form and condition of central Dublin visually expresses the cultural, political, and economic history of the city", they say, echoing Lewis Mumford. "Despite many mistakes and errors of judgment made in demolition and replacement of buildings since the 1960s, the predominant urban form is still remarkably intact as an example of the 18th century style of civic design. The buildings, streets and squares of central Dublin provide a unique balance of moderation, intimate scale, harmony and good principles of urban design and civic environment". However, the consultants go on to say that, at present, there is no mechanism under the Planning Acts providing for area-based building conservation, as distinct from the listing of individual buildings. "In this respect, we are out of step with the more enlightened of our European partners, and the introduction of amending legislation under our planning code would be a helpful step in order to promote and encourage area-based conservation".

But though the consultancy study identifies the River Liffey quays as "a central element in the structure" of Dublin's historic core and notes that the quays are now "littered with derelict, disused and underused sites", it does not put forward the riverfront for an "area revitalisation project" - presumably on the assumption that the quays are already included in an urban renewal designated area. Two such projects are proposed - for the Grand Canal Dock/ Hanover Quay area and for the Liberties/Temple Bar area which, in reality, are two quite distinct areas. In the case of Grand Canal Dock, near Ringsend, the consultants seem to have accepted the conclusions of a study of the area by the Society of Chartered Surveyors, which suggested that redevelopment - mainly for residential uses - would be unlikely to get off the ground unless an estimated £17 million was invested by the public sector in site development works, infrastructural services and environmental improvement. The canal basin and surrounding land - covering an area of over 70 acres, much of it publicly-owned through CIE and the Dublin Gas Company, represents "a major resource [of] untapped potential" and its redevelopment for a range of residential and leisure uses "could provide a major stimulus to the economic revitalisation of Dublin's Inner City".

The consultants are at one with Bord Failte in identifying "heritage themes" as an important focus in the new growth area of cultural tourism. "The Viking and Medieval area of Dublin (including the Liberties) have potential in terms of a wealth of archaeological features and artefacts, including the remains of the street pattern of medieval times", they say - overlooking, for a moment, the fact that much of this street pattern has already been destroyed by dual-carriageway schemes. "With the growing interest worldwide in cultural tourism, these resources could offer a diverse base for the expansion of tourism ... which could provide welcome full-time employment for a range of skilled and semi-skilled workers". They cite the Jorvik Centre in York and the Viking Museum at Roskilde, in Denmark, as examples of what can be done, adding that both of these facilities "earn substantial tourism revenues". Their report also notes proposals for a permanent Viking exhibition centre in Dublin's medieval city as well as the establishment of an archaeological excavation as a tourist attraction.

The report is particularly positive about the Temple Bar area, describing it as "one of the last fragments of the central area which gives a picture of Dublin city before the Wide Streets Commissioners replaced its medieval street pattern with the spacious formality of Georgian streets and squares". Its charm, the consultants say, "lies in the jumble of architectural styles and the relationship of buildings within a maze of cobblestone streets and laneways". Long earmarked for the southern section of CIE's planned "transportation centre", which would have consumed almost four acres of its fabric, the Temple Bar area is developing into "a Left Bank with great character" (in the words of Bord Failte's tourism development plan) and the consultants say that there "seems to be a strong body of opinion that the area is worth protecting" - a view shared quite strongly by the Taoiseach, Mr Haughey. Indeed, at a public meeting organised by the Dublin Crisis Conference just prior to the 1987 general election, he declared that Temple Bar was "one of the most important, traditional, historic, attractive and interesting parts of Dublin, which has to be refurbished and kept, and I wouldn't let CIE near it". Perhaps more than anything else, it was this unambiguous declaration by the man who would shortly assume power that sounded the death-knell for CIE's plans for the area.

Not surprisingly, Mr Haughey's view is endorsed by the consultants who recommend that - along with the Liberties - the Temple Bar area should be developed "as a focus of cultural activity during Dublin's designation as Cultural Capital of Europe in 1991 and, subsequently, as a permanent cultural enterprise centre", as suggested in a submission from the locally-based Temple Bar Development Council. "With a view to establishing the conservation and restoration of the Temple Bar area, the following decisions should be implemented", the consultants say. "Firstly, CIE should dispose of its property holdings in this area. Secondly, Dublin Corporation should remove the proposed Transportation Centre objective in this area from the 1988 Draft City Development Plan. Thirdly, a large proportion of the existing buildings within the Temple Bar area should be retained and refurbished, following a detailed inventory of building stock condition. The basic street pattern and fabric should also be retained. Fourthly, opportunities for redevelopment should be clearly identified. Fifthly, a development plan (action plan) should be prepared with the emphasis on cultural and tourism potential to provide a coherent framework for the development and conservation of the area. Finally, in order to stimulate the economic revival of this area, the financial incentives available under the Urban Renewal Act 1986 and the Finance Act 1986 should be extended immediately to include the entire Temple Bar area".

However, while this sounds very positive, there are dangers inherent in what the consultants have in mind. For a start, and quite unaccountably, they suggest that the task of restoring CIE's substantial property holding in the Temple Bar area should be given to Arlington Securities, the British property company which has reached agreement in principle with CIE on the proposed shopping centre/bus station scheme behind Bachelors Walk and Ormond Quay. Apart from the fact that Arlington has quite enough on its plate in terms of planning and site assembly on the north bank of the Liffey, this idea runs counter to Bord Failte's firm view that CIE's properties should be sold off in separate lots to private owners who would undertake their restoration or redevelopment. The tourist board's approach reflects the recommendations made to Mr Haughey by an informal Dublin Heritage Group which he set up in 1988 under the chairmanship of travel trade "baroness" Gillian Bowler. Its main advantage is that a sale in separate lots would give some of CIE's existing tenants the opportunity of buying their buildings, thus retaining at least a vestige of the lower value uses which have contributed so much to the character of Temple Bar. The consultants, however, take the view that while the existing traders have brought new life to the area, "the favourable comment that this has attracted reflects the potential rather than the actuality of Temple Bar". In other words, they seem to be accepting as inevitable a transformation to higher value uses, with rents to match - just like what happened in the Covent Garden area of London. Bord Failte, on the other hand, places the emphasis on a mixture of commercial and residential development "including, in particular, cheaper and middle market restaurants" to help ensure life in the area for up to 15 hours a day. Certainly, the last thing Dublin needs is for Temple Bar to be transformed into a twee version of Grafton Street, groaning with "designer shops".

Dublin Corporation planners are already working on the preparation of a local area action plan for Temple Bar, concentrating in the first instance on the buildings which deserve to be listed for preservation as well as identifying the many derelict sites in the area which require redevelopment. But if the area is to be developed as an "urban village", which is what it really is, there will have to be a strong residential component. "One Thousand People in Temple Bar" is a goal which award-winning architect John Tuomey believes is not only desirable, but attainable too. As elsewhere in the city centre, the upper floors of many buildings in the area are substantially vacant or underused and they could be converted, quite economically, into flats. Indeed, when *The Irish Times* carried a report in February 1989 on a feasibility study to create eight flats on the upper floors of a large warehouse on the corner of Cecelia Street and Temple Lane, the architect who drew up the scheme, Shelley McNamara, received over 120 inquiries from people who expressed an interest in living in the area. The Government has also amended the package of urban renewal tax incentives to reduce - though not entirely eliminate - its inherent bias in favour of new development as opposed to conservation, and commercial rather than residential uses. In doing so, the Minister for Finance, Albert Reynolds, was obviously responding to appeals made by Senator David Norris and Professor Frank Convery, among others, that the package should be altered to make it more attractive economically to retain rather than replace historic buildings. As a result, people who undertake the restoration of buildings of "significant scientific, historical, architectural or aesthetic interest" within the designated urban renewal areas will be able to write off 50 per cent of the cost of repairs against their tax liability. This will help to "make conservation pay", thus preserving worthwhile buildings, and since it is specifically targeted at owner-occupiers, it should also contribute to the cause of revitalising the city.

But there are other obstacles standing in the way. Even at the most basic level, many streets in the city centre are not cabled for multi-channel television, so potential residents would have to pay a special fee to Cablelink if they wanted a service. The streets are also clogged with commuter cars and a rigorously-enforced disc parking regime, giving priority to local residents and traders, would need to be introduced before people who have cars would consider moving into the inner city. "In order to bring more life back into the heart of Dublin - especially young single people and married couples - the city's overall environment would need to be upgraded", said the Dublin Crisis Conference *Manifesto for the City*. "This should flow from a recognition of sections of the inner city as genuinely residential areas entitled to certain standards that would apply to the suburbs in regard to traffic management, provision for children and the elderly, noise and pollution control and a crackdown on such nuisances as gaming parlours, seedy nightclubs and bars with late-night extensions. There would also need to be an increase in the proportion of expenditure on such essential services as paving, lighting, cleansing and law enforcement. There must also be a commitment to improve the lot of those already living there - notably the residents of Corporation flat blocks. Apart from an upgrading of their environment, the provision of a much greater and more varied range of employment opportunties in the inner city is essential. The identification of jobs appropriate to their qualifications or skills needs to be done in conjunction with the residents themselves, or by community leaders, but these opportunities could include industrial, commercial and service-type employment - the latter offering perhaps the most viable option''. Effective leadership is required, as well as investment, but it is in this crucial area that Dublin really fails. According to Professor Convery, this is at least partly due to a "systemic weakness" in our structure of local government. "It does not allow an elected politician to emerge as a leader who can define a sense of vision, put together the necessary coalitions and obtain the necessary financial and public support to carry out a long-term programme. All of the great restoration projects in the U.S. have depended for their success upon such a leader. However, it is only fair to add that other powerful political leaders in the U.S. have achieved awesome destruction. We experience 12-month mayors, often of great ability, who can achieve little more than symbolic gestures. It is not the role of the city or county manager to define aspirations for the future, or to develop the political support necessary to bring them to fruition. Nevertheless, in the Irish system, the attitude, skill and enthusiasm of the manager or town clerk is critical. Without active support from this quarter, very little can happen''.

Since 1979, Frank Feely has occupied the key post of Dublin city and county manager. A career bureaucrat, he started working for Dublin Corporation in 1949 as a clerk, straight from school in Synge Street, acquired an accountancy qualification and worked his way up through the ranks until he reached the very top - where he could remain until May 1996, when he is due to retire. He is a great man for public relations gestures. The "I Love Dublin" campaign, the annual street carnival, the James Last concert in College Green and the Dublin Millennium were all originated by him - some would say to divert attention from the more serious issues facing the city. But the Millennium did generate a great wave of goodwill for Dublin, making ordinary people more aware of the city's value even if it didn't seem to have much impact in changing the policies being pursued by the Corporation. Gregarious, avuncular and immensely plausible, at least to the uninitiated, Mr Feely behaves as if he is the city's real Lord Mayor, sometimes even wearing his own gown of office (as town clerk), and his apparently limitless appetite for attending receptions, functions and official openings is legendary. Every year, he paints a picture of some well-known landmark in the city (the Ha'penny Bridge, the O'Connell Monument etc), to be hung on the railings of St Stephen's Green for the annual "People's Art" exhibition. He also enjoys singing such notable ditties as "Dublin in the Rare Oul' Times", banging it out as good as the best of them.

"Frank is a very defensive character", one city councillor was quoted as saying in an *In Dublin* profile of Mr Feely in February 1988. "He has the Corporation view of the world. He looks upon the conservation groups as his enemies. Frank sees himself as enlightened, but really he is part of this Corporation school himself. He has a genuine sense of the city, but his ability to transform this into policy, that is a different question". Indeed, this writer recalls attending the official opening of North Earl Street as a "pedestrian precinct" in December 1980. The Corporation had installed short lengths of PVC piping in holes in the ground at the end of the street to indicate that it was closed to traffic and, to improve the look of street - at least for the official opening - there was the usual array of park benches and shrubs in tubs. This writer suggested to the city manager that the Corporation should do a proper job on the street by re-paving it wall-to-wall, eliminating the distinction between the footpaths and the carriageway. But Mr Feely said there were all sorts of problems, such as drains and under-street basements, which would make this very difficult, if not impossible, and it would also prove very costly. However, it is surely the job of a city manager to solve problems such as these.

Mr Feely presides over a large bureaucracy which one senior civil servant described as "the most hidebound institution in the State", with an almost inate inability to take decisive action. It is the roads authority for the city as well as the sanitary authority, the housing authority and the planning authority - probably in that order. Each department has its own priorities and, quite often, these are in direct conflict with each other. For example, one senior official of the parks department was totally unaware of the road engineers' plans to take up to 25 feet off the southern end of Harold's Cross Park, with the loss of at least 12 mature trees, until this writer informed him that the scheme had been included in the draft city development plan. Ironically, the parks department is Mr Feely's particular favourite (because its work wins so much popular approval) and it has often been called on to ameliorate some of the damage done by the roads and traffic department. Thus, we have St Audoen's Park, on the edge of the High Street dual-carriageway, with neo-Gothic gateways made out of limestone street setts; or the Millennium Garden beside City Hall, with the exposed party wall of the Sick and Indigent Roomkeepers Society, blocked up fireplaces still visible, as its bizarre backdrop; or the new Peace Garden at the splayed junction of Christchurch Place and Nicholas Street, which merely underlines the loss of any sense of urban enclosure in what was once the heart of the medieval city.

Frank Feely's failure to have the Corporation's destructive road plans re-examined sits uneasily with his professed concern for the city; indeed, it has taken a Government-appointed consortium of consultants to whittle these plans down to size. Mr Feely's lack of action on this front is also in marked contrast with the decisive role played by Joe McHugh when he took over as city manager of Cork in 1974. On Mr McHugh's desk was a consultancy report which recommended a whole network of new roads in the city, some of them running on stilts along the quays of the River Lee. However, rather than blindly accepting that this was the way to proceed, Mr McHugh concluded that it would result in far too much damage to the fabric of the city and, in any case, there was no money available to finance such grandiose schemes. So he pushed forward with a major land use and transportation study of the Cork region meeting with the new consultants every month to make sure that they were still on the right track, and the end-result became popularly known as the "LUTS" plan. And though new roads and bridges were proposed, some in the inner city area, the damage to Cork's architectural fabric was kept to an absolute minimum; indeed, under LUTS, only *six* buildings in the city were to be demolished for road-widening. In Dublin, the Corporation's hit list runs into hundreds, yet Mr Feely still denies that the city is being destroyed.

Many of the improvements made in recent years only happened after the Corporation had been cajoled, persuaded and even goaded into taking action by conservation and community groups. For example, until bricklayer Matt Byrne, of An Taisce, produced a report called "Our Granite Pavements", highlighting the importance of this aspect of the city's heritage, the Corporation's standard response to the idea of re-laying cobbled setts on the streets was that this simply couldn't be done. Assistant city manager Sean Haughey said women wearing stiletto heels might fall on the cobbles and the Corporation could be held liable for any injuries. A similar "reason" was advanced by the roads and traffic department when it came to re-cobbling Crane Street, outside the Guinness Hop Store, to prepare it for the installation of a steel sculpture by American artist Richard Serra. Though the city manager had agreed to do it, the project was held up on the advice of a senior engineer, who pointed out that tarmacadam was now the standard street surface in Dublin and if the Corporation deliberately laid "non-standard" limestone setts and a motorist was to have an accident on a dark wet night which could be attributed to the fact that the street had been cobbled, the Corporation might have to pay out substantial damages. Thankfully, these reactionary views have now been silenced and the Corporation is making quite a good job of re-cobbling some of the streets in the Temple Bar area.

One of the root problems is that the wrong sort of people are in charge. The Corporation is run by officials and its professional staff - planners, architects and, to a much lesser extent, engineers - play second fiddle. At meetings of the City Council's planning committee, for example, only the manager of the planning department, John Prendergast, and the principal officer, Paddy Quinlan, sit at the head of the table, alongside the councillors. The chief planning officer, Gay McCarron, and other senior planners sit in chairs ranged along the wall of the committee room and, rather like Victorian children, they only speak when they're spoken to. Significantly, it is Mr Prendergast, rather than Mr McCarron, who has taken upon himself the task of piloting the draft city plan through the planning committee, advising the councillors which pieces of land should be re-zoned or which buildings they should list for preservation. At the first meeting to consider listings, not one photograph illustrating any of the buildings involved was shown to the councillors despite the fact that it is their function, rather than that of the officials, to make the city plan. And when former Lord Mayor Carmencita Hederman complained that this made it impossible for the councillors to reach a rational judgment on which buildings should be listed for preservation and which should not, Mr Prendergast said that they should be prepared to accept the recommendations made by the planners - sight unseen.

Some of the most qualified Corporation planners have become so demoralised by the way things are run that at least four of them have applied for voluntary redundancy. They include Michael Gough, a former president of the Irish Planning Institute (IPI), whose tenure as planning officer in Waterford in the late 1970s led to the first-ever listing of interiors for preservation, and Tony Mulhall, who has completed a highly-regarded architectural conservation course in the University of York. This was reflected in Mr Mulhall's learned contribution to the IPI's journal, *Pleanail,* on the issue of finding a suitable form for the development of Dublin's medieval city. He saw the picturesque clocktower of the Christchurch Square office scheme on High Street as a disturbing indication of the trend in contemporary architecture towards "a Utopia of the past" through the "prosaic re-use of historic forms". Instead, he called for the adoption of an authentic "conservation ethic" which would embrace the preservation of old buildings as well as the construction of "recognisably modern" buildings which would, at the same time, be "compatible" with their context. "The creation of a new three-dimensional form and the articulation of the external space without offending the integrity of the site or denying the origin of the building is the challenge for architecture in the historic city today", Mr Mulhall declared. For him, however, this has remained an academic exercise; because of the way in which the planning department is run, he has been given no role in meeting the challenge.

The determination of the officials to retain complete control is also reflected in the fact that Dublin no longer has a City Architect; after the premature retirement of Daithi Hanly in 1965, the post was split in two - Housing Architect and Civic and Amenities Architect - and, in neither case, is there a direct reporting relationship with the city manager. Now, under pressure from the Royal Institute of the Architects of Ireland and in the hope of heading off the establishment of an Inner City Renewal Authority, the Corporation's management are to reinstate the more prestigious post of City Architect. However, it is likely that the first occupant of the post will come from inside the ranks - the present Civic and Amenities Architect, Chris Dardis, who, like Gay McCarron, has learned to live with the limitations of the system. Only when he retires will the Corporation even consider bringing in a total outsider.

The need for a City Architect with real power could hardly be more pressing at a time when so much of Dublin lies in ruins. The last time major rebuilding was required - excluding, of course, the major speculative office development boom of the 1960s and 1970s - was in the 1920s, after the city's fabric had been devastated by the 1916 Rising and the Civil War which followed. But then,

SAVING THE CITY

Dublin had a City Architect of great stature, Horace Tennyson O'Rourke, and it is to him that we owe the splendid buildings which now line O'Connell Street. Somebody of equivalent stature is now sorely needed - if only to stand up for the cause of civic design against the bureaucrats and, indeed, the planners. A City Architect would also have a role in preventing what happened, for example, to a Corporation housing scheme at the corner of Haymarket and Queen Street. The Corporation's generally excellent housing architects had designed this group of houses around an internal courtyard and the scheme was just about to go to tender when the roads engineers intervened. They revealed that the east side of Queen Street was now to be widened, rather than the west side, and their power within the ranks of officialdom is such that the tender documents were scrapped and the whole scheme was then redesigned - without the courtyard and with provision for a road "take" of about 15 feet on the Queen Street frontage. Or take the case of nearby Paul Street, where the Corporation had blocked up its entire stock of yellow-brick artisan houses, leaving them as a playground for local vandals. Originally, the plan was to demolish the lot and replace them with new houses, but then the deputy city manager and housing co-ordinator, Paddy Morrissey, had second thoughts about this and formed the view that the existing houses could be refurbished instead. The next time he inquired about it, however, he was surprised to discover that they had already been demolished, leaving nothing behind but two derelict fenced-in sites, running the entire length of the street. "My wife and I spent our first three years of married life in a house in Paul Street", one Dublin taxi driver recalled. "Everytime we pass it by now, a lump comes to our throats. We were happy there. It's such a shame that it's gone". A City Architect might have saved that little Dublin street from such a sad and capricious end. He, or she, might also have prevented the broad expanse of Blackhall Street, with its symmetrical Georgian terraces framing the Bluecoat School, from being turned into a lop-sided mess. On one side stands the stock housing solution of the 1960s - the five-storey maisonette block - and, on the other, the stock solution of the 1980s - the three-storey terrace of town houses.

The Corporation could also appoint a conservation officer to monitor planning applications affecting listed buildings in the city and to give advice to owners on how to maintain their property in good repair. Two of the Corporation's planners - Tony Muhall and John Muldowney - are graduates of the year-long conservation course at York University but, as yet, neither of them have been allocated posts in which their expertise might be of some value to the site. However, a conservation officer would need to have qualifications which go beyond academic argument. He, or she, would need to know the different mortar mixes for repointing a Georgian house as well as the finer details of sash windows and glazing bars. Many a building in Dublin has been butchered by ill-advised "improvements" in recent years - notably in the areas of pointing and PVC windows - yet there is nobody to turn to for advice, apart from the under-funded and under-staffed Irish Architectural Archive. The Corporation's planning department did produce a series of leaflets on the restoration of listed buildings in 1987 - 20 years after the first listings were made - but some of the advice they contained was strongly disputed by An Taisce, which called for their withdrawal. The leaflets, which were compiled by former chief planning officer Charles Aliaga Kelly, are now out of print and there is apparently no intention of re-issuing them, even in an amended form. At some stage, perhaps the National Heritage Council will establish a central information office, headed by a suitably-qualified architect to give advice to the owners of listed buildings in Dublin and elsewhere.

In dealing with plans for development in the city, the Corporation suffers from a failure of nerve. Having permitted all sorts of atrocities in the past and been roundly attacked for their decisions, some of the senior planners now seem to have retreated to a fall-back position in which the blandness of Georgian pastiche is welcomed and audacious modern architecture is shunned like the plague. This was certainly the reaction to a startling scheme by Des McMahon, of Dublin architects Gilroy McMahon, to build a sophisticated glass-and-steel office block alongside a faithful reconstruction of No. 29 Clare Street, the once fine mid-18th century town house which was reduced to a ruinous state over the past 15 years. Forgetting for the moment the fact that the Corporation itself occupies two of the ugliest buildings in Dublin, the pair of bunkers at Wood Quay, city councillors joined in the fray, some of them insisting that only a rust-coloured brick building would be acceptable. Yet this was the sort of compromise with mediocrity which turned Lower Mount Street into a grim-walled canyon and transformed almost half of Harcourt street into a Hollywood set of "Georgian replicas". The Corporation would be better off trying to get some of the small things right - like the paving of the city's streets. Instead of coherent design standards, there seems to be a different formula for every setting. Some footpaths are re-paved in standard concrete slabs with granite kerbing, which is the right way to do it, but others are done in a mixture of grey and red-dyed concrete setts, like a down-market version of Grafton Street. Worst of all is Dawson Street, where the footpath has been widened through the quite arbitrary addition of concrete cobbles between the paving slabs and the granite kerbstones. These substandard finishes are defended on the basis that there's not sufficient funds to do a proper job. However, there seems to be no problem finding money to buy pubs and pull them down for the sake of gaining extra road space for traffic.

Three or four years ago, the Corporation's standard response to queries about why nothing was being done to prevent O'Connell Street being transformed into as honky-tonk freeway was that shopkeepers were in business and, if they felt that plastic signs were what the public wanted, who was the Corporation to argue with them? Indeed, it was the Corporation's abject failure to stem the tide of tat in the main streets of the city centre that prompted the former Fine Gael Minister for the Environment, John Boland , to set up the Dublin Metropolitan Streets Commission in 1986, with a mandate to upgrade the main axis of the city centre, from Parnell Square to St Stephen's Green. The Corporation got the shock of its life and, though the streets commission was quickly terminated in 1987 - for purely political reasons - by the former Fianna Fail Government, the promise held out by its brief reign was to have a lasting impact on the main shopping streets. The turning point came in December 1987 when, as a result of a watertight case build up by Dick Gleeson, one of its most dedicated planners, the Corporation went to the High Court and obtained an injunction to prevent Apollo Discounts opening yet another unauthorised bargain store in O'Connell Street. For the first time in years, city centre shopkeepers could see that the Corporation actually intended to enforce the planning code and, almost overnight, it seemed that they were falling over each other in a race to install tastefully-designed new shopfronts. Similarly, it is unlikely that Grafton Street would have been re-paved to a relatively high standard if it hadn't been for the pace set, however briefly, by the streets commission.

The energy and dedication of voluntary groups in the community is also sapped by the uncaring response of the bureaucracy. One example will suffice. The John Dillon Street Association in the Liberties noticed the Corporation's commitment to "community planning" in the draft city plan and responded with a modest proposal to improve their immediate environment, thus contributing to the "rejuvenation" of the medieval city. They invited a Dutch planner to talk about the *woonerf* concept in Holland, which involves redesigning streets to give primacy to people over cars, and then got a designer to produce a scheme for John Dillon Street, providing security against car theft and "rat-running" through-traffic, a pleasant walking environment for residents and visitors alike and an attractive play space for the 125 houses in the area, none of which have gardens. The association won support from An Taisce and the South Inner City Community Development Association, and even got a promise of assistance in cash or kind from Hillview Securities, developers of the nearby Christchurch Square offices and flats complex, if the Corporation approved the plan. "In short", the association said in a letter to *The Irish Times* in February 1989, "we did all the groundwork over two years and submitted a full proposal with commercial backing to Dublin Corporation's planning, roads and traffic departments and the city manager's office last July. To date, we have not received one written response, positive or negative, despite repeated phone calls and letters''. Indeed, it was only after the association's letter appeared in the paper that the Corporation cranked itself into action, telling the residents of John Dillon Street that it had neither the time nor the money to take their proposal on board at this stage. "We didn't expect immediate approval, but why do they not talk to us? Why waste all this voluntary and enthusiastic effort? Has our proposal fallen between the em-battled positions of the various factions in the Civic Office bunkers?", asked the association.

Way back in 1967, in the Corporation's first draft development plan, the Charlemont Place/Charlemont Street area of the city was designated as "Urban Renewal Area No. 3" and, on foot of that, whole terraces of houses and shops there were demolished. Over 20 years later, it is Dublin's largest single dere-lict site, extending over five acres of land, with only a small local authority housing scheme to show for all of this "planning". The latest draft city plan designates five run-down districts of the inner city as "rejuvenation areas" - the Liberties, the Medieval City, Smithfield, Grand Canal Harbour and the Custom House Docks - but no firm indication is given on precisely how this "rejuvenation" is meant to happen. The report of the EC study consultants, with its targeting of Grand Canal Harbour and the Liberties/Medieval City, will presumably help to ensure that these areas will not lie fallow for as long as the Charlemont Place/ Charlemont Street site. Their prospects have also boosted by the belated announcement, in Fianna Fail's general election manifesto, that the urban renewal tax incentives were being extended to take in Grand Canal Harbour, Smithfield and a large chunk of the Medieval City as well as eight more provincial towns - some of them located in marginal constituencies. Curiously, such an extension of the "designated areas" had been ruled out by the Minister for the Environment, Padraig Flynn, while the Dail was debating the 1989 Finance Bill, and his own Department knew nothing about his change of heart. But then, elections provide an irresistible incentive for politicians in power to cast around for vote-catching schemes.

In the case of the Custom House Docks, things are already in hand because the Coaltion Government in 1986 set up a statutory development authority, under the chairmanship of former Corporation planner Frank Benson, to take over responsibility for this area's renewal. And even aside from the State's heavy commitment to the 27-acre site, in terms of tax incentives and promotional back-up, the authority still managed to astonish everyone by the break-neck speed at which it produced a planning scheme, invited tenders and chose a consortium - Hardwicke/McInerney/British Land - to undertake a £250 million re-development scheme, consisting of an international financial services centre, a museum and gallery complex and a hotel and conference centre, as well as cinemas, restaurants, bars and shops, and no less than 200 apartments. There was also a pledge to retain the impressive vaults of Stack C, one of the early 19th century warehouses on the site, but this has since been dishonoured because it didn't suit the construction programme. Another feature of the area which was doomed from the outset is Sheriff Street flats and, in May 1989, the Minister for the Environment directed the Corporation to "de-tenant" the entire complex, demolish the run-down flat blocks and put the site up for sale to the private sector. It would appear that the Indians are being cleared out to make way for the Cowboys, just like what happened in the London docklands.

Whether all of what is promised for the Custom House Docks site actually materialises is a moot point at this stage. But if everything doesn't fall into place, it won't for the want of carrots. From the start, the package of urban renewal incentives was geared very much in a particular direction - to underpin the redevelopment of the Custom House Docks site, even at the expense of much more needy areas. That's why the 27-acre site got its own development authority and fatter tax concessions - including a 100 per cent write-off on the capital cost of development, compared to just 50 per cent elsewhere in Dublin. True, 100 per cent write-offs were provided for in the designated areas of Cork, Limerick, Galway and Waterford - but then, they don't represent direct competition for the Custom House Docks. However, in Dublin's other designated areas, along the River Liffey quays and in the north inner city, the ceiling for write-offs was fixed at only 50 per cent. And since the benefit of the renewal incentives was extended to nearly a dozen provincial towns, a development in, say, Athlone or Wexford is more favoured than one in, say, Mountjoy Square. There was some hope, even expectation, that this discrimination against Dublin would be rectified by the 1989 Finance Bill. But the Department of Finance, which always seeks to limit the scope of tax incentives, argued that there was no longer any need to bolster the situation in Dublin. After all, several schemes had already got under way and more are in the pipeline, even under the present regime, so why gild the lily? (Stranger things have happened. In 1988, for example, the Government agreed to designate a greenfield site in Tallaght as an "urban renewal area", giving it the benefit of the tax incentives, even though there was nothing *urban* in the area to *renew*. It was purely a device to ensure that the long-delayed "town centre" scheme would materialise, at last. Immediately, the developers of a much larger regional shopping centre in Blanchardstown sought the same favoured treatment - even though this particular scheme could have an adverse impact on shopping in the city centre).

But the success of the Custom House Docks Development Authority, however well underwritten, seemed to show that a public body set up with a single purpose could achieve results. This theme was taken up by the Construction Industry Development Board (CIDB) in its strong recommendation to the Government that an Inner City Renewal Authority should be set up, to take charge of the entire area bounded by the Grand Canal and the Royal Canal/North Circular Road. The board had studied the urban renewal strategies adopted in Britain, West Germany and the United States and found that almost all of them depended for their success on the involvement of some agency outside the structure of local government. It argued that the Corporation, because it is organised along functional lines to provide a wide range of public services from refuse collection to road maintenance, was just not capable of implementing a "concentrated and integrated renewal strategy" extending over a number of years. Accordingly, the board recommended the establishment of an Inner City Renewal Authority to act as "a vehicle for the regeneration of Dublin Inner City" and, in particular, to prepare an overall renewal strategy for the area, to draw up local action plans for specific areas "in consultation with appropriate interest groups", to promote and market the inner city as a location for private investment, to hold land and carry out amenity schemes and, finally, to "co-ordinate the involvement of local communities, building societies, investors, developers and commercial interests".

The CIDB's thinking was spelled out by one of its members, Dublin architect Tony Reddy, at the RIAI's annual conference in October, 1988. Even apart from the bureaucratic nature of the Corporation and, in particular, the effect of the *ultra vires* rule in stifling initiative among its officials, he said that a body which had itself been "a major contributor to much of the decay and dereliction which has occurred in the city ... lacks credibility in encouraging others to carry out sensitive redevelopment or refurbishment schemes". An Inner City Renewal Authority, on the other hand, would be carrying none of this baggage and so would be able to "act as a vehicle for 'partnership for progress' between the public and private sectors and the local communities". As envisaged by the CIDB, the authority would consist of a chairman and eight members, with expertise in business management, property development, architecture, chartered surveying, marketing and urban design/town planning. It would also have a small staff "head-hunted" from various sectors of the public service, including the Corporation, the Department of the Environment, universities and technical colleges, on secondment from their permanent posts, backed up - where necessary - by specialist consultants. In general, the CIDB envisaged that the authority would prepare a planning scheme, or action plan, for designated areas of the inner city, such as the Temple Bar area, to provide a proper framework for urban renewal and, in each case, the public would have a statutory right to have its views taken into account. (It is worth noting that Dublin Corporation has not adopted a single "local area action plan" for any part of the city, despite the fact that the powers to do so have been available since the 1963 Planning Act came into force 25 years ago).

Initially, the Minister for the Environment was quite positive in his response to the proposal for an Inner City Renewal Authority. But at another meeting with a CIDB sub-committee some weeks later, Mr Flynn was decidedly more cautious, saying that it required further study and the board might like to look for an "internal solution", by recommending ways in which the Corporation itself could be reformed. The CIDB's chairman, property developer Robin Power, took the hint and the whole thing was long-fingered. Few seem to know what changed the Minister's mind, but it would appear that neither the Taoiseach, Mr Haughey, nor Mr Flynn (on reflection) want to establish another independent authority in the centre of Dublin, with responsibility for the entire inner city. It is an open secret that their relations with Frank Benson, at the Custom House Docks Authority, have not been exactly smooth - mainly because of Mr Benson's disconcertingly independent line and, in particular, his resistance to any political interference with the functioning of the authority. So Mr Haughey and his Ministers are quite content to continue with the existing arrangement whereby they can summon senior Corporation officials to Government Buildings and tell them, in no uncertain terms, that their sole function is to "facilitate development". As one demoralised planner put it, the Government has become "the planning authority for Dublin", dabbling in decisions on development control which are legally the function of the Corporation. Indeed, it is to the door of the Taoiseach or the Minister for the Environment that developers - especially cross-channel developers - beat a path in the hope of winning powerful political support for their schemes, even before the planners themselves are consulted. "Confidentially", Mr Flynn told an urban renewal seminar in 1988, "I have developers making appointments with me continuously, on an international basis". By leaving the threat of an inner city renewal authority dangling in the background, and making its own wishes abundantly clear, Mr Flynn and Mr Haughey can ensure that the Corporation "performs" - in the crude sense of "facilitating development".

This helps to explain why nothing was done to prosecute car dealers Linders of Smithfield for their illegal demolition of five Georgian houses on Arran Quay one weekend in January 1989. Incredibly, this started on the same day that Linders lodged a planning application for an office development on the site, and it was even facilitated by the presence of gardai who helpfully cordoned off Arran Quay - without notice - while the demolition work was under way. However, Linders believed they were doing nothing wrong; they had met with Bill Lacy, one-time principal officer for the "designated areas", and Michael Reynolds, the Ballina-born geographer who is the senior planner for the inner city, for "pre-application" discussions and were told that their scheme to replace the Georgian terrace with four office blocks would be quite acceptable in principle. At no stage, the firm maintains, was it told that planning permission would be required in advance to demolish the five houses or that some residential content should be incorporated in the proposed development. When An Taisce protested at the destruction of yet another stretch of quayfront buildings, the Corporation at first tried to suggest that the houses had been condemned as "unfit for human habitation". Later, however, it transpired that this referred only to a few flats; at least two of the houses were still "habitable" within the meaning of the Planning Acts and, accordingly, planning permission would have been required to demolish them. But when it was put to the Corporation that Linders should be prosecuted, the response was that it was "not expedient" to do so. Indeed, there was some irony in the fact that the only legal proceedings in the case were taken against Ian Lumley, of An Taisce, and Ciaran Cuffe, of the Students Against the Destruction of Dublin, who were both charged with breach of the peace when they attempted to establish whether Linders had permission to demolish the buildings. The charges - which, in Mr Lumley's case, included assaulting a policeman - were later struck out for lack of evidence.

The Corporation's accommodating attitude to development, along with the coincidental boom in the building industry, may be sufficient to stave off the threat of an independent inner city renewal authority, since the Government's sole concern is to see cranes on the skyline. The standing of the Corporation has also been boosted by the appointment of Derek Brady, a youthful and enthusiastic principal officer, as the man in charge of the inner city. Formerly in the roads and traffic department, where he tried to find a compromise solution to the Clanbrassil Street controversy, Mr Brady has shown an extraordinary degree of initiative in cutting through the red tape to facilitate developers who want to build in the inner city. He was more acutely aware than most Corporation officials of the damage wreaked by the road plans and he accepted the argument of conservation groups that little or nothing was being done to encourage redevelopment along the streets which had been devastated. In the case of Patrick Street, for example, the only plan which the Corporation had was to build seven houses on a car park site directly opposite the Iveagh Trust flats - despite the fact that this would have produced a disjointed and un-balanced streetscape. With sites in the area now fetching substantial sums - such as the £2.25 million paid for less than two acres of land at Christchurch Place - Mr Brady commissioned Corporation housing architect David O'Connor to design a complete elevation for the west side of Patrick Street, offering a vision of how it might be redeveloped with buildings of equivalent stature to the Iveagh Trust flats. And the encouraging result was that, when the site was advertised for tender in May 1989, developers were virtually queueing up to acquire it.

In general, however, the Corporation does not seem to have a clear idea of the kind of development it wants to see in highly-sensitive areas like the Liffey Quays or the Medieval City. Apart from the broad-brush zoning of the city development plan, no detailed plans have yet been drawn up for specific, identifiable districts of the city - despite the designation of five "rejuvenation areas" to be rehabilitated and renewed. It would be wrong, however, to suggest that nobody in the planning department is thinking along these lines; a lot of good ideas are floating around - but usually in the minds of planners below the top echelon who have little or no power to implement them. In the 1987 issue *Pleanail*, for example, planner Dick Gleeson conceded that the present zoning approach "is not adequately responding to the needs and potential of many grey areas within the inner city". Dubliners were even losing their "mental maps" of these grey areas, he suggested. They knew very well the locations of O'Connell Street, College Green, Grafton Street and the Quays, but they couldn't place even well-known buildings like St Patrick's Cathedral in the context of the street pattern which surrounds them. And the reason he advanced to account for this phenomenon was that nobody walked around the city's grey areas and, therefore, didn't build up a mental map of them. "The challenge and opportunity lies in trying to re-establish the same sense of place or function for those grey areas that is currently to be found in, say, Stephen's Green, Grafton Street or College Green'', he declared.

Mr Gleeson, who has done more than most to change the face of the main shopping streets, put forward the idea of breaking the inner city down into "more meaningful, manageable and identifiable areas" - a ring of zones around the central business district. "Trinity College provides an excellent blueprint of the sub-zone idea; good territorial definition, clear function, excellent environmental design and management, and conservation of its historic buildings. Car access is seriously curtailed, the pedestrian is paramount and there are extremely interesting through-walking routes", he wrote. The same could be applied to other zones, such as the medieval city centred around Christchurch, St Patrick's and the Castle, Temple Bar or Smithfield. As Mr

Gleeson noted, Smithfield has often been cited as an urban space with great potential, so far unrealised."Against all the odds, Irish Distillers have shown how a micro-environment of high quality can be achieved in an area such as Smithfield. Their building is architecturally sensitive and still modern and sophisticated, and it deserves to be matched by similar high-quality developments". (It has since been followed by the award-winning Juvenile Court, directly alongside). According to Mr Gleeson, Smithfield could become a centre for Government office relocation with the promise of "an upgraded environment, a tram connection to the Phoenix Park, input by office workers into the design of the offices, integrated swimming pool and sports facilities and, perhaps, access to the Law Society and grounds". It might equally be developed as a predominantly residential area, with the fabric of the great stone warehouses retained as impressive facades for new apartment buildings; Bolton Street College is not far away and, indeed, its submission to the EC study consultants suggested that there was a potential for 500 student flats in the vicinity. Given that McInerneys are undertaking a similar development on UCD's sprawling campus at Belfield, it should be possible to interest a developer in recycling the derelict State-owned distillery buildings on Bow Street, off Smithfield. In the report of the consultants, however, Smithfield does not feature at all. It remains a grey area with a weak "mental map".

If there was any real planning in Dublin, the Corporation would be trying to find a new role for some of the "secondary streets" in and around the central business district - like Capel street, Dorset Street, Parliament Street, Talbot street and South Great George's street - where the problems of vacant upper floors and even vacant retail space at ground-floor level are at their most acute. Capel Street, for example, has become an *ad hoc* centre for the furniture trade and it would make sense actively to encourage this trend, with incentives if necessary. Similarly, Francis Street has been developing as a focus for antiques and, here again, this could be reinforced by opening an outdoor market like London's Portobello Road or, perhaps, turning the Iveagh Markets into an antiques bazaar. Consideration might also be given to relocating the wholesale "rag trade" from South William Street to Parnell Street, where the various firms involved could be accommodated in new buildings on either side of the new dual-carriageway. This would also free the many fine houses in South William Street, currently defaced by signs and shutters, for conversion into city centre flats. And why should most of the city's nightclubs be lurking

The Juvenile Court in Smithfield by award winning architect, John Tuomey, which is one of the better buildings erected in Dublin in recent years. Smithfield, with its vast cobbled surface, offers considerable potential for urban renewal. (Photograph: Pat Langan).

SAVING THE CITY

Demolition work in progress on a terrace of Georgian houses at Arran Quay, near St. Paul's Church. At least two of the houses were "habitable", and Linders of Smithfield, who owned the property had no planning permission to pull them down. (Photograph: The Irish Times).

in the basements of Georgian houses along Lower Leeson Street, otherwise known as "The Strip"? Would it not be better all round if they were along the Liffey Quays? That's what deputy chief planning officer Pat McDonnell suggested in 1985 as an exciting possibility for Bachelors Walk but, as usual, it was not taken up by the Corporation - or anyone else.

The story is somewhat different elsewhere - especially in Berlin and Glasgow, the two European cities which have been setting headlines for urban renewal in recent years. In 1987, Berlin celebrated its 750th anniversary and, on both sides of the Wall which divides the city, the occasion was seized as an opportunity to atone for past mistakes and neglect and to make a lasting contribution to the cause of renewal. Indeed, even the once-desolate area around Checkpoint Charlie was drawn into the whole exercise, with major building and restoration projects giving new life to Friedrichstrasse, even though it's cruelly cut in two by the Wall. Unlike Dublin, Berlin was ravaged by aerial bombardment during World War II and most people would be under the impression that hardly anything was left standing after the war was over. But the truth is that only 20 per cent of the city's buildings were destroyed or damaged beyond repair and, as in many British cities, the real vandalism was perpetrated by post-war planners, with their ruthless programmes of demolition and "comprehensive redevelopment", leaving behind a legacy of highways, high-rise housing, office blocks, shopping centres and, of course, vast areas of dereliction. Mounting pressure from community groups, which culminated serious rioting in protest against official policies, eventually persuaded West Berlin's city council to take a radically different course and, in 1979, it set up the International Building Exhibition - known as IBA - with a mandate to "rescue the shattered city".

The whole ethos developed by IBA's director, Josef Paul Kleihues, was based on the post-modern idea of using architecture as an instrument for knitting the city together again. Some of the best-known names in the patheon of post-modernism - Aldo Rossi, Rob Krier, Hans Hollein and James Stirling - were brought in to "do their thing", but the focus was very much on urban planning, instead of individual architectural projects. "Every town has its own idiosyncrasies, its own history and its own conventions. Wherever this is ignored, urban culture and the city as a place to live can only deteriorate", according to Kleihues - and who, indeed, could argue with him? Thus, the thrust of IBA was to re-establish the "ground-plan" of West Berlin - the streets and the squares which gave the city its shape - and to build new buildings in sympathy with its scale and traditions. What makes this even more impressive is that the vast bulk of the new architecture consists of apartment buildings, rather than office blocks - which is in line with IBA's overall objective of returning the inner city to the people of Berlin as a place to live. And ironically, much of it was made possible by the availability of large tracts of derelict land in Friedrichstadt - just south of Checkpoint Charlie - which the city council had earmarked for a motorway scheme, now mercifully abandoned.

But IBA is not all about new buildings, or town reconstruction, as they call it; a great deal of its most valuable work has been in the area of "town repair" - the rehabilitation of run-down 19th century tenement buildings, particularly in the densely-populated Kreuzberg district. Under the direction of Hardt-Waltherr Hamer, a professor at the Berlin College of Art, this unusual programme traded under the name of STERN - a German acronym for the Careful Urban Renewal Company Ltd. - and operated in accordance with 12 guiding principles adopted by the city council in 1983. The most important of these principles were that renewal work must be planned in conjunction with the local residents and business people and it should be carried out in such a way as to preserve the building fabric as far as possible. Kreuzberg's special character was to be protected, and the confidence and trust of people living in the threatened neighbourhood had to be re-established, and no work was to proceed without an agreement between the planners and the people on what shape it should take and what its aims were. By the end of Berlin's 750th anniversary year, half of the 11,200 flats included in the STERN programme had been renovated, 30 streets and squares were redesigned, gardens were planted in 320 previously bleak courtyards and 23 day-care centres were provided as well as new shops, sports halls, cultural centres, playgrounds, parks and even children's farmyards.

Even more important than these bald figures, as Professor Hamer said, was the fact that out of "a hopeless, dead-end situation, out of resignation and opposition, a spark of hope and self-confidence and growing identification with the neighbourhood has emerged". He also had something else to say, which should be a lesson to all those bureaucrats not a million miles away from our own City Hall who view public participation in planning with the utmost disdain. "The results which have been achieved [in Kreuzberg] with the involvement of local people contradict unmistakably the prophesies of doom made by all the opponents of careful urban renewal who still claim that the participation of local people only leads to delays. The opposite is true", he declared. Of course, a lot of money was spent - the West German government is very generous in its support of West Berlin - but money alone, as we have seen, doesn't solve urban renewal problems if there is no vision, leadership and political commitment to back it up. Those vital ingredients were very much a part of the Berlin approach, which is why what has been achieved there is an example to the world. As Bertoldt Brecht put it in the 1920s: "There is one reason for preferring Berlin to other cities - because Berlin is constantly changing. What is bad today can be improved tomorrow".

Paris, on the other hand, hardly needs improvement. It remains the quintessential European city, knocking everywhere else into a cocked hat. But Paris has also become the *capitale d'architecture*, with an amazing array of great projects, most of them initiated by President Francois Mitterrand. Indeed, ever since he was first elected in 1981, Mitterrand has been planning new monuments to embellish a city which has long been the epitome of grandeur. All over Paris, his patronage is producing sensational new buildings, such as the pyramid at the Louvre, the "people's opera" at the Bastille and the arch at La Defence, and the scale of these projects - as Arthur Gibney has said - "would convince even the Bourbon kings that the city of Paris is still in safe hands". Mitterrand is, of course, following in the footsteps of Louis XIV and Napoleon III who both left their mark on the city, transforming it into "the France of France". The grand boulevards designed by Baron Hausmann undoubtedly had an ulterior motive - to assist the authorities in putting down any rebellion by providing a clear line of fire for artillery - but they were at least designed as big wide streets, lined with fine buildings, rather than big wide roads with nothing but derelict sites on either side. At the height of the controversy over Clanbrassil Street, the example of Hausmann's work in Paris was put to Paddy Meehan, principal officer of the roads and traffic department, but his response was as blunt as it was succinct. "That's all planning rubbish", he declared.

Glasgow's much-heralded urban renewal programme got under way in the late 1970s after the authorities frankly admitted that they did not, after all, hold a monopoly of wisdom. For over two decades, the city had been ruled by what Duncan Maclennan, head of Glasgow University's Centre for Housing Research, called "the most Stalinist council in Britain", which was presiding over "the most extensive attempt to implement municipal socialism this side of the Iron Curtain". Strongly committed to a relentless programme of slum clearance, the council was demolishing between 5,000 and 7,000 tenement flats a year at the height of its power in the mid-1960s, clearing the people out to ghastly high-rise housing estates in the outer suburbs. The same council also did immense damage to the fabric of Glasgow by carving it up for an inner city motorway, showing about as much sensitivity as someone hacking his way through the jungle with a machete. But reason finally dawned, and the first positive step on the road to recovery was a decision to drop plans for yet another "new town" some 15 miles from the city centre and, instead, to draft the planners into the east end, an area of widespread social deprivation not unlike Dublin's north inner city. That was the beginning of what beame known as GEAR, the Glasgow Eastern Area Renewal project, a joint venture between the city council and the Scottish Development Agency (Scotland's equivalent of our own IDA) underwritten by massive funding from the British Government.

An even more remarkable transformation has taken place right in the centre of the city, just a few blocks from the vast Victorian City Hall. This is the 70-acre Merchant City area, sandwiched between Glasgow's modest medieval cathedral and the main shopping district, and it had been blighted for years by another of the city council's "comprehensive redevelopment" schemes. But instead of pulling down its varied stock of buildings, mostly dating from the 19th century, the council's planners began to see the area's real potential for a conservation-based renewal project. As usual, it took others to point the way. A chap called Iain Mackenzie is credited with getting the ball rolling eight years ago when he took a lease on the wood-panelled office of the cheese market and turned it into the hugely popular Cafe Gandolfi. A few years later, former quantity surveyor Fraser Laurie spotted the roofless ruin of a Robert Adam-designed classical building in nearby Blackfriars Street, rebuilt it from top to bottom and opened it as a tremendously attractive city centre *auberge* - incorporating a cafe/bar, restaurant and *pension* - trading under the unlikely name of Babbity Bowster's. Both developments proved instantly successful with younger people in particular. They began to rediscover the area, just as their Dublin counterparts have flocked to Temple Bar, and the Merchant City became "the place to be", as the SDA's brochure says.

The city council's strategy for the Merchant City, as planner Jim Patrick explained, was to "convert a problem into an opportunity and turn that opportunity into a solution". Instead of wringing its hands over the dilapidated state of the area, it set about persuading developers that the vacant upper floorspace could be converted into residential use, with the aid of a package of housing rehabilitation grants (an average of £5,000 per flat) "to make the sums add up". Courage was required because there was no obvious "market" for flats in the area, but the pilot project in 1983, involving the conversion of Albion Buildings on Ingram Street, was a great success and all 23 one-bedroom flats were sold within months. Other schemes quickly followed, such as the conversion of a massive granary on nearby Bell Street into 164 flats - and, this time, prospective purchasers camped out overnight. Even more ambitious was the Ingram Square development, which takes in a whole city block. Like other parts of the Merchant City, many of the buildings here had been bought up for demolition by the city council and the block also included three cleared sites. But with the change in planning policy, the urban fabric of Ingram Square was stitched together through an imaginative combination of conversion, partial restoration and new "infill" buildings, with flats on the upper floors, shops at street level and car parking underground. And the remarkable result of all this activity in the Merchant City is that, from having a next-to-nil residential population just five years ago, there will be at least 4,000 people living in the area by 1992.

But no consideration of urban renewal in Glasgow would be complete without mentioning the tenement rehabilitation programme because, more than anything else, this has changed the face of the city. The scale of it is staggering. Literally hundreds of sooty-black Victorian buildings have been cleaned down, revealing once again their rich red or yellow sandstone facades. Since 1976, a total of 16,000 tenement flats have been refurbished and the vast bulk of this work has been carried out, not by the city council, but by 21 community-based housing associations. Ninety per cent of the cost, which works out at an average of £25,000 per flat, is met by government housing rehabilitation grants and, at the height of Glasgow's programme in 1983/84, the city was absorbing 10% of the total grant allocation for the United Kingdom and 80% of Scotland's share. Almost all the tenements are terraced four-storey buildings with shops on the ground floor and their rehabilitation depended on getting the co-operation of everyone - residents and shopkeepers alike. In most cases, this meant that each block had to be vacated for six months to a year while the work was done, with the residents temporarily rehoused elsewhere, a process that became popularly known as "decanting". And this entire programme is co-ordinated by the people themselves - a remarkable tribute to the housing association movement and its ability to transform a city. It is in this context that the Scotland's largest city really lives up to its cocky slogan, "Glasgow's Miles Better", and deserves its title as European Cultural Capital for 1990.

Within Ireland itself, new standards have been set by Galway - the uniquely attractive western capital, where there always seems to be a festival in full swing. For its size, the city has managed to attract a disproportionately large share of development activity into its urban renewal designated area, creating whole streets full of bright new shops, offices and homes. Old buildings, like the Bridge Mills, have been "recycled" for new uses and plans are being drawn up to convert more redundant stone-built warehouses into flats, restaurants and other facilities. The new buildings, by and large, are designed in sympathy with the medieval character of Galway and, in one case, a new development at Buttermilk Walk, between Middle Street and St Augustine Street, actually reinstates a medieval lane. These schemes also reflect the strong preference of Galway planner John Roche for "sharp edges" instead of the usual splays, setbacks and other compromises to facilitate traffic. Just down St Augustine Street, indeed, he is doing something that his counterparts in Dublin would never do - trying to persuade the owners of the Hynes Buildings - a hideous late-1960s office block, set back 15 feet or so - to extend it *to the front* to reinstate the old building line. Plans for the McDonagh site, off Eyre Square, where a major archaeological excavation was undertaken by the Corporation, include preserving the old city wall, which marks the western boundary of the site, rebuilding Penrice's and Shoemaker's towers as a major "theme" feature of a large shopping centre, and locating interpretive facilities in a massive 17th century bastion underground. And like other new developments in Galway, this scheme will have a substantial residential content - a total of 37 houses on the "roof" of the shopping centre. There are also plans to restore Kirwan's Lane, one of the last survivors of the city's fourteen medieval lanes, and it is expected that a suitable home will be found there for the disembodied Browne Doorway, now standing at the head of Eyre Square.

As town clerk Joe Gavin pointed out, Galway was almost uniquely well-placed to run with the urban renewal scheme. First of all, it hasn't got an "inner city", in the pejorative sense, an area plagued by problems. Secondly, the city's industries are mainly in "growth" areas and, unlike Cork, it suffered no major closures in recent years. Thirdly, though its population is only 50,000, Galway serves as a regional shopping centre for much of Connacht, with a catchment area of 175,000 extending from north Clare to south Mayo. And finally, the city benefits greatly from the presence of 7,000 students, in the university and the regional technical college. They seem to walk or cycle everywhere, which is particularly easy for students at UCG because it's right on the doorstep of the city centre, just beyond Dr Michael Browne's magnificent folly, Galway Cathedral. "They spend all their money in town, on digs and bed-sits, in the shops, pubs and eating-houses. And when they desert it every summer, they're replaced by the tourists", said local auctioneer Danno Heaslip. The aim now is to persuade the tourists to stay longer, though what's happening in Galway isn't just for the benefit of the tourists. There is a strong commitment - both within and outside the Corporation - to protect the city, in its own right, and to make it an even more attractive place to live in. Unlike Dublin, the local authority and the community are not at war with each other; the Corporation doesn't always see eye-to-eye with groups like An Taisce and the Galway Archaeological Society, but it doesn't treat concerned citizens as tiresome cranks.

As the capital, Dublin ought to be giving an example to the rest of Ireland, but the city is lagging so far behind that it can actually learn a lot from what's being done in provincial cities. In Cork, apart from devising a sensible solution to the traffic problem, the Corporation pioneered the concept of housing protection areas, where it became a firm policy to discourage encroachment from offices and other non-residential uses. Maximum use is made of a revolving fund to purchase derelict houses in key areas, such as the South Parish, carry out renovations and then sell them on to people who want homes in the inner city. A major survey was also undertaken to establish the extent of vacancy and under-use on the upper floors of shop premises in the city centre and, had money been made available, the Corporation would itself have converted some of these buildings into flats just to show what could be done. And when it came to installing a multi-storey car park on Lavitt's Quay, the Corporation didn't settle for something sterile like the grimly functional car parks in Drury Street and Sean McDermott Street. Instead, the structure was cleverly concealed by a shopping centre, with a *piazza* on the Paul Street frontage, and the entire development has brought new life into the area. The urban renewal scheme has also produced results - like the conversion of a former fire station on Sullivan's Quay into eight flats, with a shop at street level, while on South Terrace a derelict site is being replaced by a "mixed use" development of offices and flats, the best of which have fetched up to £70,000. But then, Cork has always set a headline for conservation and renewal. With a sensitive chief planning officer in John O'Donnell and a committed city architect in Neil Hegarty, it has been more fortunate than most. This does not mean that no mistakes are made; the "restoration" of the Firkin Crane building in Shandon, by the Irish Ballet Company, turned out to be a regrettable piece of butchery, the State office block on Sullivan's Quay - built with an exemption from planning control - is an atrocious intrusion, and the new shopping centre at Merchants Quay must be counted as a disappointment. But at least the fabric of the city has not been willfully wasted and the overall thrust of planning policy is in the right direction.

Waterford is also making waves on the urban renewal front and, again, it is the city's Corporation which is giving the lead. Under the quietly effective leadership of Michael Doody, the city manager, Waterford has been demonstrating what a committed local authority can do to create the right climate for investment. Indeed, over the past ten years, the Corporation has been the principal agency in the acquisition, renovation and recycling of some of the city's most important old buildings - including the Bishop's Palace, which now serves as offices for the engineering and planning departments; the Deanery, where the finance department is located; the former Friends Meeting House in Garter Lane, which it converted into a 250-seat theate, and the Methodist Church in Greyfriars, which has been transformed into a heritage centre. Waterford also fully exploits its archaeological potential, perhaps with an eye to reclaiming from Kilkenny the title of Ireland's premier medieval city. The Corporation employs a full-time archaelogist, Maurice Hurley, and he supervised a two-year "dig" on a major shopping centre site in the urban renewal designated area, unearthing remains of Viking city walls, houses and churches. Planners Gerard Sheeran and Stephanie Taheny are also involved in preparing local action plans for small, but critical, areas of the old city such as Spring Garden Alley, in consultation with the local people.

In Limerick, too, despite obvious handicaps, progress is reported. For years, the city had been left to rot, with dereliction spreading like a cancer through its core, and there seemed to be no hope of recovery. Instead of being a lady, as the song would have it, Limerick was turning into a lay-by. Then, the Corporation took a positive step by restoring some of the stone built houses on St John's Square, indicating by its action that all was not lost. This was soon followed by the Granary project, involving the conversion of a very prominent grain store off the Dublin road into an office and leisure complex. Shannon Development, conscious of the need to promote Limerick as the mid-western capital, set up its own urban renewal team to work with the Corporation, injecting much-needed marketing and business skills into the joint enterprise. But what really helped to turn things around was the appointment of Cork-born Jim Barrett as city architect. Formerly a partner in the Dublin firm of Delaney McVeigh and Pike, where he designed the first and, arguably, the most successful of the inner city housing schemes, on Meath Street, he brought with him a fresh enthusiasm for Limerick as well as a single-minded determination to revive its flagging fortunes. His goal is to re-establish a relationship between the city and the Shannon, on which it has turned its back for too long, and he was fortunate to find that this vision was shared by the award-winning Limerick-based architects, Murray O'Laoire. Already, the results of their combined efforts may be seen in the restored Potato Market, linked to a sculpture park in front of the Custom House by an attractive metal bridge, and in the plans for a civic park at nearby Arthur's Quay. Even more ambitious is Mr Barrett's scheme to restore King John's Castle, by getting rid of the local authority houses which were dumped in the middle of its medieval courtyard during the 1930s. However, instead of issuing an edict that the two dozen houses were to be demolished, the city architect personally visited every householder and promised that he would build new houses for them in the immediate vicinity of the castle if they would vacate their present homes. They all agreed, illustrating yet again that consultation with the public is much more productive than confrontation.

The Dublin Crisis Conference *Manifesto for the City*, published in January 1987, noted that public involvement in the planning process is now actively encouraged in most European countries. "In Ireland, however, public participation is minimal. Very little information is made available, usually the absolute minimum required to fulfill statutory obligations, and it is only released after the real decisions have already been taken behind closed doors. Even exhibitions of the City Development Plan, on which ordinary people are entitled to make their views known, seem designed more to confuse than inform, with their indecipherable maps full of colours, dots and lines. If there was a genuine desire to involve the public, the planners would make their plans intelligible, with simple explanatory leaflets, widely circulated, and good publicity in the newspapers, on radio and television. And instead of reviewing the Development Plan for the entire city, a mammoth task which is usually undertaken once every decade, the plan should be reviewed on an area-by-area basis once every five years; this, too, would help to ensure greater public participation".

However, when it came to one of the most critical issues to face Ireland for years - the aid which we might expect to get from the EC Structural Funds and what this should be spent on - there was virtually no public participation in the decision-making process. The first thing that happened, allegedly to save money on travelling expenses, was the abolition of the nine regional development organisations which, whatever their faults, at least had some degree of democratic accountability. But the Department of Finance belatedly realised that the EC Commission would be insisting on at least on a veneer of consultation and partnership at regional and local level, so it established an entirely new set of seven "sub-regions" where, in each case, it supplied the chairman for a "working group" consisting entirely of officials drawn from Government Departments and the relevant local authorities to cobble together "plans" for each region. Each working group was supplemented by an "advisory group" consisting largely of representatives of the "social partners" - the employers, trade unions and farmers - together with a few token local politicians who would, in theory, vet the plans prepared by the working group in its sub-region. In the "sub-region" made up of Dublin city and county, this created the ludicrous situation whereby no less than four farming organisations were included in the advisory group while there was nobody to represent community and environmental interests. Simultaneously, the Department of Finance - together with the Government - was drawing up a national development plan, and it became clear that the extent to which each sub-regional plan corresponded with what the Department and the Government already had in mind was precisely the extent to which it was incorporated in the eventual plan submitted to Brussels.

This was classic "top-down" planning, with little or no role for the wider community. Indeed, the first official notice from the Department of Finance inviting submissions from the public was not placed in the newspapers until December 16th, 1988 - almost a year after the process got under way. The Department had no particular interest in hearing the views of ordinary people or the community groups which represented them, and it would have kept the whole thing under wraps but for the need to pay lip-service to the EC Commission's expressed wish for some degree of public involvement. Only those who had an inside track, like the Dublin Chamber of Commerce, were able to position themselves to take advantage of the expected bonanza from Brussels. Indeed, the chamber was the only non-governmental organisation represented on the steering committee set up to oversee the consultancy study of the Dublin sub-region and it was included, no doubt, because it is regarded as "sound", in the sense used by Sir Humphrey Appleby, of *Yes, Minister* fame. No attempt was made to counter-balance the chamber's narrow business interest with, for example, a representative of the trade union movement or someone - even a local politician - who might be said to reflect the wider public interest, as opposed to the interests of officialdom. Neither the Department of Finance nor the Government were interested in fresh, imaginative solutions to Dublin's problems and, indeed, this cast of mind was reflected in the original brief for the consultancy study which seemed to call for little more than a re-packaging of existing plans. It was only after strong representations were made to the EC Commission by former Lord Mayor Carmencita Hederman, among others, that the brief was amended - at the insistence of Brussels - to allow the consultants to look beyond what was already on the table.

"Most member States are sophisticated enough to do their own multi-annual development programmes", said one well-placed EC Commission source, in a frank assessment of the situation. "But our experience with the Irish authorities in recent years is that they're addicted to aid for its own sake, almost like a Third World country, without really considering what it's being spent on or why. They never listen, never read anything we send out and never contribute anything to the quality of the debate. They're passengers all the way and, if they go on like this, they'll end up on the sidelines, like clowns at a circus". A claim by Maire Geoghegan-Quinn, Minister of State for European Affairs, at the Fianna Fail ardfheis in February 1989 that "local elected public representatives already have a full role in drawing up the regional integrated programme for the EC Structural Funds" was hotly contested by the Community Workers Co-Op, which has been to the fore in fighting for a real community input into the Euro-plan. "A plethora of community groups, professional associations, environmental groups etc, as well as local elected representatives, have been highly critical of the planning process and the secrecy surrounding it. Are these all liars? Is Fianna Fail the final pillar of honesty, protecting us from those who would wish to mislead us into believing that political hands are keeping a tight grip on the purse strings while political mouths try to convince Europe that they're not?", asked the co-op's Gearoid O Riain, in a letter to *The Irish Times*.

Later, after the Government launched its national development plan in a blaze of publicity on March 31st, it transpired that none of the plans prepared at sub-regional level - with the single exception of the Dublin consultancy study - were being sent to Brussels. And because there was no plan for Dublin, or any of the other sub-regions, the consultancy study was simply shelved; it no longer had any status, except as a reference document. It also became clear that the various sub-regional working groups and advisory groups were ad hoc creations, set up purely "for the purpose of this consultation", and they would have absolutely no role in overseeing the implementation of the plan - unless, of course, the EC Commission insisted on it. This came as a major shock to many of those who had been involved in the preparation of sub-regional plans. "The clear impression of everyone involved was that we were producing the basis for an operational programme for the region, and the last thing I expected was that this was going to end up in a bin in the Department of Finance", said one reliable source. Instead, with the active participation of Padraig O hUiginn, powerful Secretary of the Taoiseach's Department, the Mandarins of Merrion Street assisted the Government in culling the bits and pieces they liked from the seven sub-regional plans and incorporated these elements into the national plan, discarding the rest. Apart from the Dublin consultancy study, the only other documents submitted to Brussels were various operational programmes dealing, on a sectoral basis, with such areas as roads, tourism, sanitary services and industrial development. And though these programmes contain the details which flesh out the broad outline of the national plan itself, only one of them - the roads programme - had been published at the time of writing. Indeed, the Government's strategy was to keep the operational programmes under wraps to the greatest possible extent until after the EC Commission made its decision on what would, or would not, be funded - by which time it would be too late for anyone in the wider community to have any influence on the outcome. (Under the joint programme for Government agreed between Fianna Fail and the Progressive Democrats, the sub-regional working groups and advisory groups - however inadequately structured - are to be retained to monitor progress on the implementation of the national plan in their areas).

In Holland, by contrast - as the *Manifesto for the City* pointed out - there is a strong tradition of decentralised decision-making from the State through provincial and municipal tiers down to district level - and this applies particularly to urban renewal. Amsterdam has eleven urban renewal districts and, in each of them, there is a district project group - paid for by the city administration - with its office in the locality. The group chairman is responsible to the local aldermen, but each group operates independently, even in its dealings with the city council. One key element in this system is that all district project groups must have the agreement of local residents to their schemes in order to secure government funding. Indeed, the architect of any new housing scheme is actually chosen or approved by the residents themselves. Dublin Corporation has made some strides in this area with the various refurbishment schemes for inner city flats. This programme started in Fatima Mansions where the local community, brought together initially to fight back against the drugs menace, organised an effective community association to demand an upgrading of their housing and environmental conditions. Indeed, it was as a result of Davy Byrne, assistant city manager in charge of the community and environment department, going to Britain with them to see for himself how similar flats were being refurbished that the whole concept was even tried here in Dublin. And the best thing about the way it's being done is that the Corporation has opened an office on the site, with a housing architect assigned to consult with individual residents on their requirements. Local people, according to David Donnison, professor of town planning at Glasgow University, "are the principal asset of the area and working with them, responding to their perceptions of the problem and getting money into their hands wherever you can - for them to decide how to use - is enormously important. Simply to ride in like the US cavalry, without consulting and working with local people, and to ride off again in a couple of years time, will leave nothing much behind".

The Royal Institute of the Architects of Ireland (RIAI), in its submissions to the EC study consultants, said funding for urban regeneration "must encompass the development of an open participatory planning process" and it suggested that Dublin should be designated as "European Capital for Community Planning" for the full duration of the EC-funded development programme. It called for the establishment of a network of "community planning committees" throughout the city and county, each serving a population of around 50,000 and co-terminus, where possible, with established neighbourhood and ward areas, such as the old borough of Rathmines. "Based on successful models such as the Dutch Project Groups, a typical community planning committee would have 51% representation from the local community, with the remainder consisting of officials and public representatives drawn from the local authority. Each committee should have a local planning shop or office, permanently staffed and with a full professional/ technical service directly under its control and management'', the architects said. "All area action plans and neighbourhood studies should be initiated at this level, and the planning committee should have a direct input into the planning policy and objectives of both borough and strategic planning for Dublin".

SAVING THE CITY

Another sure way of achieving a greater degree of active public involvement in the planning and design of the city's environment would be to promote the concept of housing associations. As we have seen, community-based housing associations played a major role in transforming Glasgow, particularly in the area of tenement refurbishment; indeed, it is impossible to imagine how urban renewal on the scale achieved there would have happened without them. In Ireland, however, housing associations and co-operatives are very unusual birds. Some small suburban housing schemes were built by co-ops, instead of private developers or the local authorities, and more might have been done if a few of the co-ops hadn't failed for one reason or another - a fact which senior Corporation officials have cited repeatedly when they were accused of having a negative attitude to the whole concept of housing co-operatives. Under the present legislative framework, there is very little support for co-ops as a vehicle to for the provision of housing and, predictably, the building societies have not been terribly helpful either. The only role for co-ops is in the narrow field of providing for the needs of certain categories of people - the disabled, for example - and, to help them to do this, they receive financial aid from the Department of the Environment. NABCO - the National Association of Building Co-Operatives - has been arguing for a wider and more role over the past few years but, so far at least, its appeal appears to have fallen on deaf ears.

The Crisis Conference manifesto warned that the manner in which local government in Dublin is to be reorganised seems likely to reinforce public alienation from the planning process. "Dividing the city and county arbitrarily into four administrative units, each with a population of around a quarter of a million will not bring local government closer to the people, still less ensure that their voices will be heard. The fact that Tallaght, which was supposed to be a self-contained 'new town' with 90,000 inhabitants, is to be lumped together with Lucan/Clondalkin and subsumed into the new county of 'Belgard' while Blanchardsown becomes part of county of 'Fingal' illustrates just how arbitrary the boundaries are. [They were drawn up, in fact, by former Taoiseach Garret FitzGerald on the basis of what he called "natural areas" - the north county, the area between the River Liffey and the foothills of the mountains at Rathfarnham and the area stretching from there to the sea, which is to become a new "county" of Dun Laoghaire. But though all of this was announced in 1985, it has yet to be implemented]. If there is to be real local government in the Dublin area, the administrative units would need to be much smaller, preferably catering for a population of between 50,000 and 100,000. Thus, not only would Tallaght have its own district council, but we would also see the revival of local government in the old boroughs of Rathmines and Pembroke - abolished in the late 1930s - as well as other parts of the city. (Although the Manifesto did not say so, any devolution of power to local level should be accompanied by a return of domestic rates or some other form of property tax; more than anything else, Fianna Fail's decision to abolish these rates in 1978 has emasculated Irish local government).

"As a first step towards a more democratic, locally-based system of local government, there is surely a case - even on a pilot basis - for decentralising public information facilities on the development functions of local authorities in the areas of planning control, roads, parks and housing. This could be operated as part of a "one-stop" district office, including manpower/employment functions, to advise intending developers and community interests on plans for the area. Within designated urban renewal areas, as in Holland, such an office would have executive as well as information functions, with the aim of involving the community in the renewal project and securing their agreement to what is being planned [as already happens, to an extent, in the refurbishment of flat complexes like Fatima Mansions]. Funds for such schemes would be provided, through the local authorities, under the little-used Section 14 of the 1963 Planning Act or by ploughing back the revenue from planning charges so that it is actually used for planning purposes.

"Other measures needed to encourage public participation and make the planning process more democratic would include amending the Planning Acts to ensure that Bord Pleanala cannot over-ride a local authority Development Plan, except by going through the normal process laid down for material contraventions of the plan. There is also a need to make Bord Pleanala inspectors' reports publicly available, since people are entitled to know the basis on which the board makes its decisions - and whether these decisions are being made capriciously, against the advice of the board's own inspectors, and to amend the planning regulations to ensure that anyone making representations to a local authority on a particular planning application is actually informed in writing of the decision, in time to make an appeal to Bord Pleanala, if necessary. Consideration should also be given to abolishing the fees for planning appeals, since their existence represents a considerable burden for residents' associations, conservation interests and other voluntary groups, while raising only minimal revenue for the board.

"Bord Pleanala's independence from direct political interference must be safeguarded if there is to be public confidence in the impartiality of appeals process. At the same time, however, it must be recognised that the board is operating in a policy vacuum because of the virtual absence of guidelines to inform its decisions. To overcome this problem, there is an urgent need for the Minister for the Environment to make much more use of the powers available under the 1976 Planning Act to issue policy directives to the board and to the local authorities. (Over the past 12 years, this provision has been used only twice - in 1982, to ensure that the consideration of plans for new shopping centres took into account the impact they would have on established retail outlets and, in 1988, to ensure that provision is made in new housing schemes for the burning of smokeless fuels). But if the planning system is to become more democratically accountable, many more policy directives will be needed on such matters as urban-generated rural housing, the preservation of buildings, the designation of conservation areas and other pressing issues. Finally, the exemption from development control enjoyed by the State and other public bodies, under Section 84 of the 1963 Planning Act, must be brought to an end. It would probably raise constitutional problems if the State was required to seek planning permission for a development from a local authority, just as it would be quite ludicrous to insist on a local authority applying to itself. The crucial change needed to allow the public a meaningful role in commenting on, or objecting to, developments planned by State bodies would be to bring them within the ambit of the third-party appeals procedure, thus permitting concerned citizens to have the matter at issue determined by Bord Pleanala".

The Crisis Conference manifesto also outlined a philosophy for sensitive urban renewal. "It has already been seen in Dublin, as elsewhere, that massive commercial developments are fraught with problems, invariably erasing any sense of the original urban fabric and often making a negative contribution towards the goal of creating a living city. Large-scale redevelopment by the public sector is little better, mainly due to the 'megascale' at which planning occurs, removed from the reality of people's lives", the manifesto declared. "Historically, cities developed through a myriad of small investment decisions by the private sector - shopkeepers, small industrialists, even householders - and it would seem that the key to revitalising the city lies in restoring the climate in which small-scale development can re-emerge as the dominant growth force. The main advantages of such an approach are in the retention of a human scale, the provision of a diverse environment, the commitment of investors to particular areas and the opportunity for a greater number of citizens to participate in decisions affecting their quality of life. The main obstacles include the price of building land, the workings of the market, the blanket form of land-use zoning and the unwillingness of financial institutions to lend money for investment in 'low value' uses or areas".

Three years ago, in a memorable address to the RIAI's annual conference at the Dunadry Inn in Co Antrim, Seamus Heaney reminded his audience that whenever they build a new building, they are "in a profound, metaphorical sense recreating the world". Architects have an awesome responsibility, not only to design worthwhile new buildings which will add to rather than detract from the city's streets, but also to conserve and recycle the best of what we have inherited from the past. However, not even the architects know the nature or extent of this legacy because, as the RIAI has pointed out, there has not been a survey of the city's architecture for decades. "Dublin does not have a comprehensive record of the buildings and assemblies of buildings which give it its character", the institute said in its submission to the EC study consultants. Accordingly, it proposed that a street-by-street, building by-building survey should be undertaken by an expert group drawn from the Corporation, the Office of Public Works, the Irish Architectural Archive, An Taisce and the RIAI itself. Their job would be to compile "a graphic record of the pysical fabric of the City of Dublin", using drawings and rectified photography, supplemented by a written record of the history of individual buildings and groups of buildings. And all of this would serve as a resource base "against which the conservation, rehabilitation and development of the city can be measured". Sadly, however, the institute's proposal does not figure among the projects recommended by the consultants.

What is missing, above all, is any vision of the city. There was only one period in Dublin's history when this vital ingredient was present, and that was during the reign of the Wide Streets Commissioners, when the city acquired its Georgian grandeur. "There is apparently no modern equivalent to the sense of patronage which engendered the great parks, the market places, the fountains and the majestic tree-lined avenues of the Georgian epoch", wrote architect Richard Rogers in the London *Times* in July 1989. "John Nash's Regent's Park is in one respect nothing but an enormous developers' housing estate. But it is also a progressive, daring and, of course, beautiful piece of urban planning. Its realisation required determination and vision. Today, the little planning that does go on is administered by bureaucratic planning authorities; a negative force with extensive powers of refusal and delay, but entirely lacking the will or the resources to take creative steps to improve the dire condition of our environment".

However, there is something coming up which should galvanise us all into action. The Taoiseach, Mr Haughey, as he put it rather pompously in a letter to the Lord Mayor in December 1988, has "arranged" for Dublin to be designated as European Cultural Capital for 1991, in succession to Glasgow. However, when Maire Geoghegan-Quinn, Minister of State for European Affairs, was asked on RTE radio what was being planned to celebrate this honour, she talked exclusively in terms of "events" of one sort of another - classical recitals, art exhibitions, rock concerts and the like - entirely missing the point that *it is the city which is the event*. Concerts, recitals and exhibitions are fine in themselves, but how can they be staged against the backdrop of a decaying city? Perhaps the Minister of State hopes to find a latter-day Potemkin, who will design suitable sets to mask all of the derelict sites along the Liffey Quays. As things stand, grave concern is being expressed in artistic circles about the planning for 1991 and the absence of any attempt, so far, to involve a whole spectrum of people and organisations who would have something worthwhile to contribute.

"Hanging up a few banners and organising a few special events and concerts will simply not be good enough", said Ian Lumley, planning spokesman for An Taisce, in a letter to *The Irish Times*. "More than anything else, the city must make itself fit for international exhibition. The time for action is now, and the initiative must come from Government level".

Once again, however, it looks as if we will be making an exhibition of ourselves in 1991. Mr Haughey, who "arranged" the cultural year for Dublin, could not have been considering it when, in April 1989, he intervened personally to block plans for the restoration of the crumbling curvilinear range of glasshouses at the National Botanic Gardens in Glasnevin. These superb buildings were designed and built by Richard Turner, the great Victorian iron-master, and they are regarded as so important architecturally that they were chosen to represent the 19th century in the definitive postage stamp series on Irish architecture through the ages. Over the past 15 years, however, the cast iron of the glasshouses has literally been falling apart as a direct result of official neglect. After their condition was highlighted by *The Irish Times* in 1983, action was promised by the then Coalition Government, but this was limited to an architectural survey. Since then, the Office of Public Works, which is responsible for the maintenance of State-owned buildings, sought to get funding for the restoration of the buildings from the European Community and, later, from the National Lottery, but these efforts proved unsuccessful. Finally, in February 1989, the project was included in a package of OPW conservation schemes, with a total value of £3.5 million. A sum of £370,000 was to have been spent in 1989 and staff at the gardens had already removed most of the plants in the expectation that work would be starting soon when the Taoiseach ordered a report from the Minister for Agriculture, Michael O'Kennedy, because of fears that the overall cost could exceed £4 million. Yet what is the alternative to restoration? In the case of the Turner glasshouses, as they now stand, the only alternative is collapse.

Notoriously, Dublin is a city of talk, not a city of vision, and even as it disappears before their eyes Dubliners remain largely oblivious, singing pub ballads about the "rare oul' times" with an almost manic fervour. Even those who express a vague concern about the city's future seem to think that somebody else - An Taisce, the Living City Group, the Dublin Crisis Conference - is minding the store and there is no real need for them to get involved. Doubtless, this has a lot to do with the defeat of idealism, and even of rational argument, in the great battle for Wood Quay nearly ten years ago, which left scars on the civic psyche. The people of Dublin thought they could save the Viking site. They wrote letters. They lobbied TDs and councillors. They marched through the streets in their thousands, with bands and colourful banners. And they elected a new City Council, with a majority committed to their cause. But officialdom still prevailed against the will of the people, and the pair of slit-windowed blockhouses which the Corporation built on the site serve as a permanent symbol of the triumph of bureaucratic power. (If the officials had any shame, they would be trying to make amends by holding an architectural competition for the second phase of the Civic Offices, with a brief to reinstate terraces of four - and five-storey buildings both on Wood Quay and Winetavern Street to conceal the bulk of the bunkers. And if they had any initiative, they would have entered into a "sale-and-leaseback" agreement with a developer to build the second phase before the urban renewal tax

Grafton Street, paved and pedestrianised...one of Dublin Corporation's achievements after years of prodding.(Photograph courtesy of Dublin City Centre Business Association)

The north-east pavillion of the Custom House, James Gandon's masterpiece which is being superbly restored by the Office of Public Works in time for its bicentenary in 1996. (Photograph by Frank Fennell, courtesy of the OPW).

incentives run out in May, 1991).

The story of Wood Quay is well told by Thomas Farel Heffernan in his recent book, and he concludes that the reason why the people of Dublin lost had everything to do with the fact that the real power in Irish local government resides with paid officials, rather than elected representatives. He ends his book by recalling an encounter with the Corporation's PRO, Noel Carroll, in the rotunda of City Hall where Dublin's official seal *Obedientia civium urbis felicitas* - the obedience of the citizens is the happiness of the city, "probably

The Old Palm House, centrepiece of the curvilinear range of glasshouses in the National Botanic Gardens, Glasnevin. The glasshouses, probably the most important Victorian buildings in Ireland, are decaying because the Government won't spend the money required to restore them. (Photograph: The Irish Times)

the most totalitarian motto adopted by any body of government anywhere" - is set in the stone floor. "That's the city motto?" [Heffernan remarked]. 'Yes', he [Carroll] replied with a content smile, 'that's what it's all about'".

Nevertheless, it is surely significant that no less than 100 groups and organisations throughout the city, crossing all barriers of social class and particular interest, saw fit to subscribe to the Citizens' Alternative Programme for Dublin, in response to what the Government seemed to be planning for the city. The 16-point programme drew support right across the spectrum, drawing together - for the first time - the "community" lobby, the "environment" lobby and the "poverty" lobby, with signatories ranging from the Ballymun Community Coalition to the Upper Leeson Street Residents Association, the Larkin Unemployed Centre to the Royal Institute of the Architects of Ireland. Essentially, it represents a distillation of the views expressed by a wide cross-section of the public on what the priorities should be for investing aid to the city from the EC Structural Funds - and, not surprisingly, these priorities are quite different from those of the Government and the Department of Finance. Like so many other submissions, the Citizens' Alternative Programme (see Appendix 5), identifies the whole transport issue as central to the future of Dublin, strongly urging that "the over-riding priority for investment ... must be given to public transport, as opposed to catering for the private car". The EC study consultants also seem to favour public transport, but this preference is not reflected in the recommendations they make, nor is it borne out by the Government's allocation for Dublin under the national development plan. Public transport is to get a total of £36 million and roads £212 million, or six times as much. And when the Taoiseach was asked if he didn't believe that the best way to relieve traffic congestion was to provide commuters with an efficient public transport system, he replied: "You just can't get them out of their cars". But then, as Deirdre Kelly put it: "Just ask yourself the question - when was Charlie Haughey last on a bus?"

Other cities are no longer making the same mistakes. Manchester has invited tenders from the private sector to design, build and operate a light rail transit system which would, initially, run from Altrincham to Bury through the streets of the city centre, linking up the two mainline railway stations for the first time since they were built in the Victorian age. Birmingham, which was raped by roads in the 1950s and 1960s, is now planning to follow Manchester's example. Even Los Angeles, a city designed around the automobile, is so strangled by traffic congestion that it's toying with the idea of light rail transit - or even a metro. Florence has banned the cars that used to choke its historic centre, and Stockholm looks as if it will become the first capital in Europe to charge commuters for the privilege of driving into the city - at the rate of 25 kronor (almost £3) per car. And the Swedes have calculated that if this new source of revenue was used to cut public transport fares, traffic entering the city centre by road could be reduced by up to 35%. Mr Haughey is either unaware of these developments or he believes that Dublin is such a peculiar place that we couldn't even begin to think along similar lines. And yet, at the Dublin Crisis Conference meeting before the general election in February 1987, he declared that the principles set out in the *Manifesto for the City* "are totally acceptable to us, to me". Among these principles were that public expenditure should be re-allocated "to give priority to public transport, traffic management, pedestrians and cyclists rather than to roads which damage or destroy the fabric of the city".

SAVING THE CITY

Dublin has now reached a turning point in its history, the point at which it will either be saved or destroyed altogether. With the city development plan review reaching a critical stage, the county plan review about to get under way in earnest and the expected bonanza from the European Community's Structural Funds, the decisions made within the next 12 months will make or break it. "In looking to the future of this city, we are at a changover time", Dublin architect Loughlin Kealy told the RIAI's Millennium conference in the Mansion House. "It is a point of instability, where we either change the nature of the development processes in the city, or we reconcile ourselves to its decay ... There is no going back. We cannot return to a more simple perception of the city or await a better time. The interdependence of the urban community, the physical fabric, the urban economy and its infrastructure is clearly visible and expressed by gathering after gathering in a way that demonstrates a powerful emerging consensus on the problems facing the citizens ... The 'crisis' of the city is now understood as a human crisis, rather than just a serious technical problem. The deterioration of the fabric and environment of the city is not a 'failure' as such; it is the result of the system we operate - a part-inherited, part-created system of values, perceptions and procedures, built up in culpable ignorance. The Dublin Crisis Conference called for a coalition of interests to save the city. I can't think of a better definition of citizenship"

APPENDIX ONE

Dublin City Council's roll-call votes on crucial road schemes.

(1) The "compromise proposal" for Patrick Street, New Street and Clanbrassil Street under which they would have been widened to 68 feet, but not made into a dual-carriageway - defeated by 27 votes to 23 at a council meeting in January 1988.

FOR

Carmencita Hederman (Community)
Tomas MacGiolla (Workers Party)
Gay Mitchell (Fine Gael)
Alexis FitzGerald (Fine Gael)
Mary Mooney (Fianna Fail)
Tom Farrell (Fine Gael)
Eric Byrne (Workers Party)
Sean Kenny (Labour)
Maurice Manning (Fine Gael)
Eamonn O'Brien (Workers Party)
Michael McShane (Fine Gael)
Mary Flaherty (Fine Gael)
Pat McCartan (Workers Party)
Charlie McManus (Fine Gael)
Sean Dublin Bay Loftus (Community)
Pat Lee (Fine Gael)
Tony Gregory (Independent)
Christy Burke (Sinn Fein)
Joe Doyle (Fine Gael)
Proinsias De Rossa (Workers Party)
Peter Burke (Fine Gael)
Brendan Lynch (Community)
Andy Smith (Workers Party)

AGAINST:

Sean Haughey (Fianna Fail)
Paddy Farry (Fianna Fail)
Vincent Brady (Fianna Fail)
Ned Brennan (Fianna Fail)
Bertie Ahern (Fianna Fail)
Michael Barrett (Fianna Fail)
Noel Ahern (Fianna Fail)
Alice Glenn (Independent)
Tim Kileen (Progressive Democrats)
Pat Carey (Fianna Fail)
John Stafford (Fianna Fail)
Michael Mulcahy (Fianna Fail)
Ita Green (Fianna Fail)
Olga Bennett (Fianna Fail)
Michael Delaney (Fianna Fail)
Dermot Fitzpatrick (Fianna Fail)
Tony Collis (Progressive Democrats)
Joe Burke (Fianna Fail)
Ben Briscoe (Fianna Fail)
Andrew Callaghan (Fianna Fail)
Liam Fitzgerald (Fianna Fail)
Michael Keating (Progressive Democrats)
Ivor Callely (Fianna Fail)
Ciaran O'Loughlin (Fianna Fail)
Eoin Ryan (Fianna Fail)
Michael Donnelly (Fianna Fail)
Mary Hanafin (Fianna Fail)

(Michael O'Halloran, of the Labour Party, was not present for the vote, but he had given his backing to the Corporation's dual-carriageway scheme at an earlier meeting of the council's general purposes committee).

(2) The Inner Tangent (vote taken in October 1980)

FOR

Fergus O'Brien (Fine Gael)
Eugene Timmons (Fianna Fail)
Bertie Ahern (Fianna Fail)
Jim Mitchell (Fine Gael)
Ben Briscoe (Fianna Fail)
Michael J. Cosgrave (Fine Gael)
Ned Brennan (Fianna Fail)
Alice Glenn (Fine Gael) **
Luke Belton (Fine Gael)
Tom Leonard (Fianna Fail)
Frank Sherwin (Independent)
Hugh Byrne (Fine Gael)
Vincent Brady (Fianna Fail)
Eileen Lemass (Fianna Fail)
Michael McShane (Fine Gael)
Mary Byrne (Fine Gael)
Michael O'Halloran (Labour)
Paddy Dunne (Labour)
Tim Killeen (Fianna Fail) *
Michael Barrett (Fianna Fail)
Gerard Brady (Fianna Fail)
Declan Ryan (Fine Geal)
Kit Robinson (Fianna Fail)
Joe Doyle (Fine Gael)
Vera Kinsella (Fianna Fail)

AGAINST

Sean Dublin Bay Loftus (Community)
Hanna Barlow (Communnity)
Pat Carroll (Labour)
Michael Keating (Fine Gael) *
Alexis FitzGerald (Fine Gael)
Carmencita Hederman (Community)
George Birminghan (Fine Gael)
Sean Kenny (Labour)
Mary Flaherty (Fine Gael)
Diana Robertson (Labour)
Tony Gregory (Independent)
William Cumiskey (Labour)
Paddy O'Mahony (Labour)
Tomas MacGiolla (Workers Party)
Michael Collins (Labour)
Gay Mitchell (Fine Gael)
Mary Robinson (Labour)
Mary Freehill (Labour)
Brendan Lynch (Community)
Dan Browne (Labour)

  * *Mr. Killeen and Mr. Keating are currently members of the Progressive Democrats.*
 ** *Mrs. Glenn is currently an independent.*

APPENDIX TWO

Resolution of the Dublin Crisis Conference, adopted unanimously at
the conclusion of the three-day conference in the Synod Hall,
Christchurch Place, in February 1986.

1. That this conference calls on the Government and the Dublin local authorities to
recognise and accept that the city is in crisis, and calls for radical changes in public
policy in the following areas :

(i) The development and adoption of a national regional settlement strategy which would take some of the pressure off the Dublin area.

(ii) The complete rejection of the main recommendations of the ERDO study.

(iii) The reorientation of the city's transportation system towards public transport and the cancellation of all road plans in central Dublin until a complete reassessment is carried out.

(iv) Adequate measures, including tax incentives, to ensure the conservation and rehabilitation of the architectural fabric of the city.

(v) The immediate implementation of a positive strategy for the revival of the inner city and the communities living there.

(vi) A halt to the creation of amorphous suburban areas with no social and cultural facilities or sense of place.

(vii) The urgent introduction of adequte measures to improve the city's total environment and, in particular, to reduce both air and water pollution.

(viii) Recognition of the special needs of the old and the disabled in the planning and design of the city.

(ix) Recognition of the distinct cultural and housing needs of the travellers in planning and settlement policies.

(x) Positive measures to encourage and facilitate public participation at all levels in the planning process.*

(xi) The need to amend the Constitution to make it clear that the interests of private property are subservient to the common good.

2. That this conference calls on the Government to initiate an Integrated Development Operation for Dublin, following the models of Belfast and Naples, with a view to securing from the EC sufficient funds to finance the revitalisation of the inner city.

3. That the organising committee of the Dublin Crisis Conference be mandated to consult with community and other interest groups in the Dublin area with a view to forming a broad coalition to save the city.

* *Originally, this part of the resolution also called for "an end to the practice, widespread among public officials, of treating concerned citizens as cranks". It was deleted in deference to John Prendergast, manager of the planning department, who had protested that it didn't reflect the attitude of Dublin Corporation.*

Appendix Three

Conclusion of the RIAI's Millennium Conference - "Dublin: A Positive Strategy" - October, 1988.

1. In 1975, the RIAI published the Dublin Urban Study which identified Dublin as a City in Crisis. Fifteen years later, Dublin is still a city in crisis. As architects, we have a right to say that we expect better of the urban design and management system in our capital.

2. The Dublin local authorities, or whatever body is the instrument of local government in Dublin, should:

2.1 Have a structure of public accountability and strategy at the level of the metropolitan region (ref. Cork and Glasgow experiences);

2.2 Be able to resolve environmental conflicts and controversies at a local level, be that the metropolitan or community level, depending on the issue (ref. Cork, Philadelphia, Glasgow and Belgium);

2.3 Have a management team including a City Architect and City Engineer (i.e. city and county) at the highest level alongside the City and County Manager (ref. Cork experience);

2.4 Have resources for publicly-funded infrastructural and building development as an integral part of urban strategy (ref. Paris, Glasgow and Berlin experiences);

2.5 Have sufficiently broad powers to engage in community development as an essential part of the attack on environmental deprivation and poverty (ref. Glasgow);

2.6 Place professional staff at the direct disposal of those in society who most need resources; the architectural profession inside and outside the public service has often expressed and shown its ability to have an enhanced and direct role in this regard (ref. Cork, Glasgow);

2.7 Plan its land use and transport policy on a regional basis in order to direct infrastructural development and to allocate resources to building conservation and community development (ref. Cork, Glasgow).

Appendix Four

An extract from the National Development Plan indicating the Government's priorities for the Dublin sub-region.

Sub-region 1: Dublin City and County

Expenditure on structural development included in the Development Plan which will take place in this sub-region 1989- 1993:

	Total Expenditure	Amount put forward for EC support	Support sought from EC
Transport	**£m**	**£m**	**£m**
(i) Roads: National	190.00	170.00	121.40
Non-national	22.00	7.00	4.20
	(**212.00**)	(**177.00**)	(**125.60**)
(ii) Rail and bus	36.00	36.00	16.00
(iii) Access transport (sea and air freight, sea ports and airports)	182.75	134.75	67.38
Sanitary and other local services.	53.64	43.15	21.59
Telecommunications and postal services	169.33	1.40	0.77
Energy (gas, electricity, peat)	133.60		
Industry	763.01	270.21	146.38
Tourism	60.20	60.20	32.30
Agriculture and rural development	16.25	16.03	7.25
Human resources: Education, training and employment	601.80	594.80	329.65
	2,228.58	**1,333.54**	**746.92**

APPENDIX FIVE

The Citizens' Alternative Programme for Dublin

DUBLIN CRISIS CONFERENCE
4 Old Mount Pleasant
Ranelagh, Dublin 6.
(Tel: 977410)

Mr Jacques Delors   10 April 1989
President
European Commission
200 Rue de la Loi
1049 Brussels

Dear Mr Delors,

The Irish Government has recently submitted a national plan to the EC Commission for aid from the Community's structural funds over a five-year period. The outline of this plan (but not the specific details) has just been published in Ireland and, from what we can gather, it involves a large number of investment proposal which will - if approved - have a major impact on the future of our country.

We write to you so that the Commission will be aware of the fact that, in Dublin, there is a substantial body of opinion which holds quite different views to those of the Government. Indeed, we would say that there is a wide degree of consensus in the city on what the priorities for investment should be, and this includes not just community groups and residents associations, but also voluntary and environmental groups as well as professional bodies.

Some of the groups we represent availed of the invitation from the Department of Finance (published belatedly on December 16th) to make their views known to the steering committee and consultants involved in preparing a study of the Dublin sub-region, and more would have done so if adequate time and resources had been made available. But all of the organisations whose names appear on the attached list have now come together to formulate the attached 16-point Citizens' Alternative Programme, for submission to the Irish Government and the EC Commission, setting out clearly how we feel the estimated total of £750 million in aid should be spent.

We believe that the views of the wider community have not received the attention they deserve from the consultants, the steering committee, the Department of Finance and the Government. Indeed, the level of public consultation here has been so inadequate and the contents of the Government's plan so disappointing that we feel we must take the matter to the Commission. And so, before any decisions are made on a programme for Dublin, we would appreciate an opportunity to discuss our views with the EC Commission so that you may appreciate more fully the strength of our case.

In the context of discussions on the establishment of a Community Support Framework, we would invite the Commission to send a high-level delegation to Dublin to see the city at first hand and meet the people as well as the Government. In the meantime, if you or your officials require clarification - or supporting documentation - on any point, please do not hesitate to contact us.

We would appreciate an early response.

Yours sincerely,

Deirdre Kelly.

CITIZENS' ALTERNATIVE PROGRAMME FOR DUBLIN

(1) The stated purpose of the EC structural funds is to relieve inequality in the Community, as between the richer and poorer member States. We believe this principle should also apply to how the funds are spent in Dublin, by investing in projects which would benefit disadvantaged areas - notably the inner city and the deprived outer suburbs - and not dissipate resources in the absence of an overall plan for the region.

(2) The future of Dublin is of immense national importance. It demands, in the first instance, a strategic plan for the city region, including a land use and transportation study - something which has never been done before - so that investment decisions can be rationally based. It is essential, however, that such a plan should be evolved in full consultation with the people of Dublin, to obtain the widest possible consensus on what the priorities should be.

(3) The provision of sustainable employment and a living income would be central to any effort to relive urban deprivation in Dublin, and we believe this should be done by painstakingly building and, in some cases, rebuilding the local economies of deprived areas of the city. This could be done through locally-based employment initiatives using appropriate technology, such as co-ops and enterprise centres, rather than relying so heavily on capital-intensive multinational companies.

(4) Improvements to Dublin's transport infrastructure are likely to account for the bulk of expenditure under the Operational Programme, and we firmly believe that the over-

riding priority for investment under this heading must be given to <u>public</u> transport, as opposed to catering for the private car. This is the only realistic way to relieve traffic congestion in the city as well as to improve mobility, especially for people who have no alternative - including those with disabilities.

(5) In particular, we are calling for the provision of rail rapid transit links to Tallaght/ Clondalkin, Blanchardstown/Clonsilla and Ballymun/Airport as well as the reopening of the Harcourt Street line and a <u>direct</u> connection in the city centre - either underground or overground - between Heuston and Connolly stations, to integrate with the existing DART service. Provision must also be made for cycleways as well as for water transport on the River Liffey and the canals.

(6) We are totally opposed to road-widening schemes which sacrifice the fabric of the city as well as any atempt to resurrect the Eastern By-Pass, because all of these schemes will only serve to draw more and more car commuters into the inner city, aggravating still further the present imbalance between the use of public and private transport. Alternative ways of accommodating port traffic should be investigated and, meanwhile, road investment should be confined to completing the western by-pass route.

(7) Dublin had been designated as European City of Culture for 1991 and, if this opportunity is to be exploited fully, much more attention will have to be paid to preserving the city's architectural and archaeological heritage to enhance the quality of the environment and its tourism potential. There is an urgent need for a comprehensive survey of the city's building stock as well as for incentives to encourage people to take on the restoration of listed buildings. This would also create jobs.

(8) It is essential that housing will qualify for assistance under the Operational Programme, as we believe that a special case can be made on urban renewal grounds to support voluntary and co-operative housing initiatives as well as the refurbishment of Dublin Corporation's stock of inner city flats, together with local authority housing in the suburbs. This, too, would create jobs and help spearhead an economic revival in these deprived areas.

(9) The docklands area on both sides of the River Liffey is the last remaining large tract of under-developed land in the inner city area. It is vital that this land and water space, much of which is publicly owned, is developed as a diverse and humane environment in the context of a community planning framework which is compatible with the needs of existing residents. In this context, we are opposed to further land reclamation in the inner bay area, as proposed by the Dublin Port and Docks Board.

(10) To safeguard and optimise the use of Dublin's maritime resources, we are calling

for the preparation of a coastal management plan which provides for EC water quality standards to be met in all areas where bathing has been traditional and in areas important for the shellfish industry. In particular, the installation of full tertiary treatment for sewage effluent discharges is an urgent priority. Assistance is also required to revitalise and expand recreational and educational activities as well as the fishing and tourism industries.

(11) A comprehensive air quality and energy management plan is urgently needed. Such a plan should include a five-year programme to rid the city of smog by speeding up the designation of smoke control areas and extending the infrastructure for the distribution of smokeless fuels. The city also requires a waste management plan which would place the emphasis on recycling as well as looking at the potential of incinerating the city's refuse to fuel district heating schemes instead of dumping it on landfill sites.

(12) Investment is required to conserve areas of major amenity, recreational and scientific importance in Dublin and its hinterland - preferably by taking them into public ownership or control. These would include the "green belt" areas in the outer suburbs, Howth Head and the Dublin Mountains. Special care is also needed to protect established nature reserves, such as the Bull Island and Booterstown Marsh, from intrusive development.

(13) Particular attention must be directed towards assisting groups with special needs which transcend geographical boundaries - such as homeless people and the disabled. Likewise, the culturally-specific needs of Travellers should be given due considera- tion. The main goal should be to improve the quality of life of all the people of Dublin and not just the better-off and the vested interests.

(14) Any programme of assistance from the EC which is directed towards addressing socio-economic inequality and deprivation within the Dublin region must tackle disparities in the provision of education at all levels as well as the whole issue of vocational training - for example, through the establishment of regional technical colleges in the western suburbs.

(15) To facilitate the development of a community planning framework throughout the city, adequate resources in the form of technical aid, support services and financial assistance must be put into the hands of the communities who need them most so that they can formulate their own plans. Local authority and State services should also be decentralised, through the provision of "one-stop shops" offering a comprehensive range of facilities.

(16) The EC Commission has stressed the importance of partnership with local

interests in EC-funded regional programmes. In the case of Dublin, we believe this can best be realised by abolishing the present bureaucratic arrangement (i.e. the working and advisory groups) and replacing it with a democratically accountable regional development authority for the Greater Dublin Area which would provide for genuine public participation in its decision-making process.

The groups or organisations who subscribe to the 16-point Citizens Alternative Programme for Dublin are as follows :

ACRA (Association of Combined Residents Association)
Alliance for Work Forum
ALONE
Architectural Association of Ireland
Association for Community-based Training, Education and Development
Baggot Estate Residents Association
Ballymun Community Coalition
Ballymun Community Project
Bath Avenue and District Residents Association
Beechwood Area Residents Association
Belgrave Residents Association
CAFE (Creative Activity For Everyone)
Ceannt Fort Residents Association
City Quay Community Council
Community Games Movement
Community Training Collective
Community Workers Co-Operative
Concerned Parents Against Drugs
Cyclefolk (Dublin Cycle Campaign Group)
Donabate Parish Council
Donnybrook Trust
Dublin Bay Environment Group
Dublin Civic Group
Dublin Crisis Conference
Dublin Council of Trade Unions
Dublin Green Movement
Dublin Resource Ceentre
Dublin Travellers Education and Development Group
Earthwatch Dublin
East Ranelagh Residents Association
Eccles Street Restoration Association
Family Resource Centre, St. Michael's Estate
Finglas West Tenants Asociation
Friends of Medieval Dublin
Get Tallaght Working Co-Operative Society
Grand Canal Basin Working Group
Grapevine Arts Centre
Greenfield Park Residents Association

Harcourt Terrace Defence Association
Hill Area Residents Association (Ranelagh)
Inchicore and Kilmainham Heritage Society
Iona and District Residents Association
Irish Georgian Society
Kenilworth Residents Association
Land Life Ireland
Larkin Unemployed Centre
Liberties Association
Living City Group
Loughshinny and District Development Association
Lourdes Youth and Community Services
Marino Residents Association
Maritime Institute of Ireland Environment Committee
Meadowbrook Residents Association
NATO (National Association of Tenants Organisations)
North Centre City Community Action Project
North Great Georges Street Preservation Society
North Wall Community Association
An Oige Environmental Group
Options Unlimited
Palmerstown Community Council
Pembroke Road Association
Portobello Residents Association
Ranch Residents Association (Inchicore)
Rathgar Residents Association
Regional Studies Association (Irish Branch)
RESCUE (Clanbrassil Street)
Rocheshill Protection Asociation
Royal Institute of the Architects of Ireland
Rush Community Council
Saint Vincent's Trust, Henrietta Street
Sandford Residents Association
Sandymount and Merrion Residents Association
Sculptors Society of Ireland
Sean McDermott Street and District Community Association
Sheriff Street Action Group
Skerries Marine Watch
South Inner City Community Development Association
Students Against the Destruction of Dublin
An Taisce, Dublin City Association
An Taisce, Dublin South County Association
An Taisce, Dublin South West Association
An Taisce, Dun Laoghaire Association
An Taisce, Fingal Association
An Taisce, National Council
Tallaght Community Council
Tallaght Welfare Society
Temple Bar Development Council
Tenters Residents Association

TIDE Emigration Research and Action Group
Tosach Training and Development Centre
Threshold
Union of Students in Ireland
Unemployment Alliance
Upper Leeson Street Area Residents Association
Voluntary and Statutory Group, North Inner City
Voluntary and Statutory Workers, Clondalkin·
Wadelai Residents Association
Westland Row Community Council
Women and Planning Group

Bold type indicates "Umbrella" organisations representing a number of affiliated groups with a substantial combined membership.

APPENDIX SIX

Extract from the Fianna Fail - Progressive Democrats' Programme for Government, published in July 1989:

Planning Compensation

The compensation provisions of the Local Government (Planning and Development) Act, 1963, will be amended so as to exclude the possibility of compensation where planning permission has been refused because the proposed development would contravene the zoning requirements of the land in question. This amending legislation would not contain any exemptions for existing landowners or for persons who acquire land through inheritance, except where the zoning is changed adversely to the interest of the property owner after acquisition, e.g., residential to agricultural.

Select Bibliography

Blackwell, John, and Convery, Frank J., eds., *Replace or Retain? - Irish Policies for buildings Analysed* (Resource and Environmental Policy Centre, University College Dublin, 1988).

Blackwell, John and Convery, Frank J., eds., *Revitalising Dublin - What Works?* (Resource and Environmental Policy Centre, University College Dublin, 1988).

Boland, Barry, et al, *Grand Canal Docks Feasibility Study* (Society of Chartered Surveyors in the Republic of Ireland, 1988).

Brunton, Mark; Convery, Frank J. and Johnson, Anne *Managing Dublin Bay* (Resource and Environmental Policy Centre, University College Dublin, 1987).

Byrne, Matthew, et al *Our Granite Pavements* (An Taisce Dublin City Association, 1987).

Cahill, Gerry, co-ordinator, *Dublin City Quays: Projects* (School of Architecture, University College Dublin, 1986).

Construction Industry Development Boad, *Annual Report 1987-1988.*

Davy Kelleher McCarthy, Reid McHugh and Partners, Stokes Kennedy Crowley, *GreaterDublin Area Development Programme: Preparation Study* (unpublished, 1989).

Feely, F.; Prendergast, J., and McCarron, E.G., *Dublin City Draft Development Plan* (Dublin Corporation, 1987).

Griffin, Dean Victor, et al, *Manifesto for the City* (Dublin Crisis Conference Committee, 1987).

Heffernan, Thomas Farel, *Wood Quay; The Clash Over Dublin's Viking Past* (University of Texas Press, 1988).

Ireland: National Development Plan 1989-1993 (The Stationery Office, March 1989).

Kelly, Deirdre, et al, *Dublin Crisis Conference - A Report* (Dublin Crisis Conference Committee, 1986).

McLoughlin, Michael, *Secondary Streets* (Dublin City Centre Business Association, 1988)

Lawlor, Liam; Gorman, C. T. and O'Reilly, L.P. *Eastern Region Settlement Strategy 2001* (Eastern Regional Development Organisation, 1988).

Lumley, Ian, et al, *Georgian Dublin: A Policy for Survival* (An Taisce Dublin City Association 1985).

Mishan E.J., *The Costs of Economic Growth* (Penguin Books, London).

Mumford, Lewis, *The Culture of Cities* (Secker and Warburg, London, 1938).

O'Sullivan, P. and Shepherd, K. *A Sourcebook on Planning Law in Ireland* (Professional Books, 1984).

Pearson, Peter, et al, *Dublin - The Temple Bar Area* (An Taisce Dublin City Association, 1985).

Sugrue, Una, co-ordinator, *Temple Bar Study* (Temple Bar Study Group, 1986).

The Plan for Dublin - A Strategy for Modern Urban Renewal (The Workers Party).

Towards an Inner City Policy for Dublin (Society of Chartered Surveyors in the Republic of Ireland, 1986).

Wright, Lance and Browne, Kenneth, *A Future for Dublin* (Architectural Review, London, 1975.

INDEX

Abbey Street, 67, 76, 97
ACRA, 40,
Adam, Robert, 151,
Adelaide Hospital, 117,
Albion Buildings, 151,
Alexandra College, Earlsfort Terr., 118,
Altrincham, 170,
Amiens Street, 65,
Amsterdam 20, 159,
Annes Street, South, 119,
Apollo Discount, 137,
Archaeology Ireland, 120,
Architectural Review, 24, 25,
Ardee Street, 42,
Arlington Securities, 67, 97, 128,
Arran Quay, 59, 104, 142, 147,
Artane, 29,
Arthur's Quay, 156,
Arundel, Liam, 22,
Athlone, 140,

Babbity Bowster's, 151,
Bachelors Lane, 67,
Bachelors Walk, 67, 68, 69, 97, 128, 147,
Baggot Street Hospital, 117,
Baggot Street, Lower, 35,
Bailey, Michael, 86,
Bailey, Thomas, 86,
Balbriggan, 79,
Ballsbridge, 36, 102, 108,
Ballyfermot, 29, 50, 76, 123,
Ballymun, 73, 74,
Ballymun Community Coalition, 169,
Barcelona, 27,
Bardun Estates Ltd., 88, 90,
Bargaintown Ltd., 104,
Baron Hausmann, 150,
Barrett, Jim, 155, 156,
Barry, Jim, 85,
Bastille, 150,
Bath, 20,
Beckett, Samuel, 24,
Bedford Tower Block, 115,
Beggars Bush Barracks, 24,
Belfast, 85, 99, 116,
Belfield, 17, 145,
Belgard Inn, 74, 75,
Belgard, 161,
Belleview Buildings, 55,
Bell Street, 151,
Benburb Street, 29,
Benson, Frank, 90, 139, 142,
Berlin, 147, 148, 149,
Berlin College of Art, 148,
Binns Bridge, 16,
Birmingham, 170,
Bishop's Palace, 155,
Bishop's Street, 22, 38,
Black Church, 22,
Blackfriars Street, 151,

Blackhall Place, 59,
Blackhall Street, 135,
Blackrock By-Pass, 56,
Blanchardstown, 65, 76, 83, 84, 98, 140, 161,
Blayney, Neil, 73,
Bloom, Molly and Leopold, 108,
Bluecoat School, 135,
Blue Lion Pub, 54,
Boland, John, former Minister & TD, 40, 86, 137,
Bolton Street, 53,
Bolton Street College, 145,
Bonnybrook, 101,
Booterstown Marsh, 57, 58,
Bord Failte, 127, 128,
Bord Pleanala, 80, 88, 89, 90, 91, 95, 98, 103, 112, 162, 163,
Bovale Developments Ltd, 86,
Bowler, Gillian, 128,
Bow Street, 23, 25, 145,
Brady, Derek, 143,
Bray, 64,
Brecht, Bertoldt, 149,
Breen Kelly Architects, 110,
Brennan & McGowan, 80, 87, 88, 89, 96,
Brennan, Ned, 45,
Briargate, 80,
Bride St., 20, 52,
Bridgeford Street, 34,
Bridge Mills, 152,
Briscoe, Ben, 27, 40, 52,
Britain, 140,
British Labour Government, 73,
British Land, 20, 32, 139,
Browne, Dr. Michael, 153,
Browne Doorway, 153,
Brussels, 159,
Buchanan, Colin, 59
Build magazine, 29,
Bunch of Grapes, The, 44, 47,
Bunratty Folk Park, 20,
Burke, Joe, 40,
Burke-Kennedy, Doyle & Partners, 72, 103,
Burke, Ray, Minister & TD, 80, 81, 87, 88, 89, 90, 95,
Bury, 170,
Buttermilk Walk, 153,
Byrne, Davy, 160,
Byrne, Matt, 132,

Cablelink, 129,
Cafe Gandolfi, 151,
Caffrey, Oliver, 103,
Camden Street, 66,
Capel Street, 53, 145,
Carroll, Noel, 21, 49, 168,
Casino at Marino, 22,
Castleknock, 16,
Castle Street, 21, 114,
CBD, Central Business District, 16, 51, 58, 61, 63, 65,
Cecelia Street, 129,
Century Communications, 108,
Central Fire Station, 22,

INDEX

Central Hotel, 119,
Charlemont Plalce, 138,
Charlemont St., 16, 138,
Chapelizod by-pass, 52, 59,
Checkpoint Charlie, 147, 148,
Cherry Orchard, 74,
Chesire Report, The, 27,
Christchurch Cathedral, 144,
Christchurch Place, 21, 46, 51, 132, 143,
Christchurch Square, 134, 138,
Church of Ireland, 120,
Church Street, 52, 53,
CIE, 48, 49, 64, 67, 70, 126, 127, 128,
CIF, 36, 89, 102,
CII, 36, 37,
Citizen's Alternative Programme for Dublin,
    169, 170, see also Appendix Five.
City Archaeologist, 120,
City Architect, 134, 135,
City Centre Business Association, 98,
City Council, 26, 35, 37, 38, 40, 45, 47, 48, 52, 57, 110,
City Hall, 21, 45, 71, 115, 132, 133, 168,
Civic and Amenities Architect, 134,
Civic Offices, 22, 48, 113, 120, 138, 166,
Clanbrassil Street, 40, 43, 44, 45, 46, 47, 51,
    52, 53, 62, 70, 143, 150,
Clanbrassil Street Residents & Traders Association 40,
Clare Street, 107, 108, 136,
Clarke's Free School, Dr., 112,
Clondalkin, 16, 50, 60,65,66, 76, 79, 83, 85, 161,
Clonee, 29, 88,
Clonliffe Road, 57,
Clonsilla, 100,
Clontarf, 40, 102,
College of Marketing & Design, 22,
Combat Poverty, 28,
Commissioners, of Public Works, 107, 120
Committee on the Price of Building Land, 94,
Community Workers Co-op, 158,
Construction Industry Development Board, 140, 141, 142,
College Green, 130,
Connolly Station, 50, 65, 67,
Convery, Frank, 16, 26, 129, 130,
Coombe, The, 42, 120,
Cooke, Michael, 89,
Cook Street, 29,
Coolock, 29,
Corcoran, John, 88,
Cork, 82, 99, 132, 140, 153, 154, 155,
Cork Street, 42,
Commarket, 31, 123,
Corporation Flat Blocks, 130,
Costello, Declan, 80,
Costs of Economic Growth, The, 33,
Craig, Dr. Maurice, 107,
Crane Street, 133,
Criteria Developments Ltd., 88,
Cromien, Sean, 100,
Cruickshank, Dan, 20,
Cuffe, Ciaran, 143,

Cuffe Street, 36, 52,
Cutlural Capital of Europe 1992, 127, 152,
Custom House, 20, 22, 24, 114, 168,
Custom House Limerick, 156,
Custom House Docks Development Authority, 90, 140, 142,
Custom House Docks site, 68, 138, 139,
Dame Street, 51,
Dardis, C.P., 109, 134,
Darndale, 74,
DART, 50, 51, 56, 57, 59, 60, 64, 67, 68, 69, 70, 74, 75, 76,
Davis King, 108,
Davy Kelleher & McCarthy, 52, 57, 68, 115,
Dawson Street, 137,
Deanery, The, 155,
De Blacam & Meagher, 21,
Declaration of Amsterdam, 107,
Delaney McVeigh and Pike 155,
Delaney's Pub, 37,
Denmark, 126,
Derelict Sites Bill, 122,
Desmond, Barry, MEP, 56,
DGS, Ltd., 112, 113,
Dillon Street Association, The John, 137, 138,
Dodder Valley linear park, 91,
D'Oliers Street, 22, 35,
Dollymount Strand, 74, 75, 123,
Dolphin's Barn, 51,
Dominican Convent Eccles St., 108, 118,
Dominick Street, 29,
Donabate, 82,
Donnison, David, 160,
Donnybrook, 102,
Doody, Michael, 155,
Dorset St., 16, 145,
Drogheda Corporation, 112,
Drogheda Grammar School 112, 113,
Drudy, P.J. 35, 64, 65,
Drumcondra, 16,
Drumcondra By-Pass, 57,
Drury Street, 154,
Dubhlinn, 28,
Dublin Bay, 56, 76, 86, 102, 123,
Dublin Bus, 68,
Dublin Castle, 114, 144,
Dublin Chamber of Commerce, 36, 157,
Dublin Crisis Conference, 27, 69, 96, 117,
    122, 127, 129, 156, 163, 166, 170, 171. See Appendix Two.
Dublin Civic Group, 26
Dublin City Centre Business Association, 60, 167,
Dublin City Development Plan, 57, 71, 107, 110, 127, 156,
Dublin County Council, 73, 74, 76, 84, 85, 86, 87, 88,
Dublin County Development Plan, 80, 81, 84,
Dublin Gas Co. 126,
Dublin Heritage Group, 128,
Dublin Metropolitian Streets Commission, 137,
Dublin Port & Docks Board, 56,
Dublin Port, 58, 59,
Dublin Transport Authority, 49, 50, 62, 63,
Dublin Transportation Study, DTS, 56, 69,
Dukes Street, 119,

INDEX

Dundrum, 16, 66,
Dun Laoghaire, 57, 95, 123, 161,
Dutch Project Groups, 160.

Eastern By-Pass, 56, 57, 58,
Eastern Region Settlement Strategy 2001, 81,
Eccles Street, 107, 108, 110.
EC conference centre, 114,
EC, European Community,
28, 29, 52, 62, 64, 65, 70, 71, 79, 83, 85, 114, 115,
119, 123, 125, 157, 158, 159, 160, 164, 166, 170.
EC Structural Funds, 16, 49, 65, 156, 158, 169, 171,
Ellis Quay, 38, 39, 59,
Embankment City, 74, 75,
Environment, Dept of, 36, 56, 86, 91, 141, 161,
Environment, Minister for the, 81, 89, 92, 94, 137, 139, 163,
ESB, 113,
ERDO, 81, 82, 83, 99, 118,
ERDF, 115,
European Architectural Heritage Year, 107,
European Captal for Community Planning, 160,

Farel Heffeman, Thomas, 168,
Fatima Mansions, 160, 162,
Feely, Frank, 18, 21, 23, 36, 62, 130, 131, 132,
Fennell, Frank, 168,
Fettercairn, 85,
Fianna Fail, 26, 80, 85, 89, 90, 92, 137, 139, 158, 159, 162,
Finance Act 1986, 128,
Finance Bill 1989, 139, 140,
Finance, Department of, 64, 100, 107, 115,
140, 157, 158, 159, 170,
Fine Gael, 47, 80,
Fingal, 161,
Finucane, Marian, 18,
Fishamble Street, 114,
Firkin Crane, 154,
Fitzgerald, Garret, 40, 63, 81, 89, 161,
Fitzwilliam Street, Lower, 113,
Florence, 99,
Flynn, Padraig, Minister & TD, 86, 90, 92, 98,
94, 95, 96, 97, 112, 139, 141, 142,
Foras Forbartha, 85,
Fortunestown, 88,
Four Courts, 24,
Francis Street, 145,
Frankfurt, 27,
Free Church, Great Charles Street, 121,
Freeney, Fr. Paul, 96, 97,
Friedrichstrasse, 147,
Friends Meeting House, 155,

Gaiety Theatre, 20,
Gallagher, Cyril, 85,
Gallagher, Matt, 88,
Galway, 82, 97, 99, 120, 140, 152, 153,
Galway Archaeological Society, 154,
Galway Cathedral 153,
Gandon, James, 20, 168,
Garter Lane, 155,

Gavin, Joe, 153,
Geoghegan-Quinn, Maire, 158, 165,
Georges Quay, 68,
Gibney, Arthur, 17, 150,
Gilbride, Jim, 185,
Gilmartin, Tom, 97, 98,
Gilroy McMahon, 136,
GEAR, (Glasgow Eastern Area Renewal Project), 150,
Glasgow, 99, 117, 147, 150, 151, 152, 161, 165,
Glasgow University, 150, 160,
Glasgow University's Centre for Housing Research, 150,
Glasnevin, 24, 165,
Gleeson, Dick, 137, 144, 145,
'Gold Coast', 1102,
Golden Lane, 20,
Good Times Bar, 38, 39, 41,
Gough, Michael, 134,
Grafton Street, 128, 137, 144, 167,
Granary, The, 155,
Grand Canal, 15, 140
Grand Canal Dock, 126,
Grand Canal Harbour, 138, 139,
Grange Developments, 87, 88, 94, 96,
Grangegorman, 101,
Great Georges St., South, 119,
Greek Street, 29,
Greene, Michael, 102,
Green Cinema, 32,
Green Property Company, 88, 98,
Gregory, Tony, TD, 39,
Griffin, Dean Victor, 46, 47, 48,
Griffith Avenue, 56, 57, 58,
Guinness, Arthur, 120,
Guinness Hops Store, 133,

Hamer, Prof, Hardt-Waltherr, 148, 149,
Hanly, Daithi, 134,
Hanover Quay, 126,
Ha'penny Bridge, 131,
Harcourt Street Hospital 118,
Harcourt Street Railway Line, 66,
Harcourt Terrace, 72, 103,
Hardwicke, Property, 139,
Hardwicke Place, 111, 121,
Harold's Cross, 16, 45, 52, 66, 131,
Harrods, 118,
Harrington Bannon, 108,
Hartstown 76,
Haughey, Charles J, Taoiseach, 26, 40, 46,
48, 90, 127, 142, 165, 170,
Haughey, Sean, Ass. City Manager, 38, 39, 45, 46,
47, 48, 133,
Haughey, Alderman Sean, 47,
Haymarket, 135,
Health, Department of, 117,
Heaney, Seamus, 164,
Heaslip, Danno, 153,
Hederman, Alderman Carmencita, 36, 45, 133, 158,
Hegarty, Neil, 154,
Henrietta Street, 113, 116, 121,

INDEX

Herbert Street, 88.
Hibernia, 80,
High Court, 87, 89, 91, 94, 109, 137,
High School Harcourt St., 118,
High Street, 52, 120, 132, 134,
Hillview Securities, 138,
Holland, 138, 159,
Hollein, Hans, 148,
Hollywoodrath, 88,
Holy Faith Convent, Dominick St., 118,
Housing Architect, 134,
Howth, 64,
Howth Tram, 69,
Hueston Station, 50, 65, 67,
Hurley, Maurice, 155,
Hynes Building, 153.

ICS Building Society, 22,
ILAC, 34,
In Dublin, 21, 47, 52,
India, 27,
Industrial Development Authority, 17, 101,
Ingram Street, 151, 152,
Inner City Relief & Port Access Route, 57,
Inner City Renewal Authority, 134, 140, 141,
Inner Tangent, 23, 36, 37, 51, 52, 54, 55, 57,
Institute of Professional Auctioneers & Valuers, 100,
International Building Exhibition, 148,
Irish Architectural Archive, 30, 136, 164,
Irish Ballet Company, 154,
Irish Congress of Trade Unions, 89,
Irish Constitution, 96,
Irish Distillers, 145,
Irish Life, 68, 76,
Irish Planning Institute, 89, 92, 93, 97, 134,
Irish Sweeps, 108,
Irish Times, 23, 25, 33, 41, 42, 44, 54, 55, 77, 78, 81,
   90, 96, 105, 110, 129, 138, 147, 158, 165, 166, 169.
Iveagh Baths, 21,
Iveagh Trust Flats, 143, 144,

Jacob's biscuit factory, 22,
James Joyce, 25,
Jameson Distillery buildings, 24, 25,
Jervis Street, 67,
Jervis Street Hospital, 117,
Joint Oireachtas Committee on
Building Land, 94,
Joint Programme for Government July 1989,
159, see also Appendix Six.
Jorvik Centre, 126,
Juvenile Court, 146,

Kealy, Loughlin, 171,
Keating, Michael, 110,
Keenan, John, P., 80, 89
Kelleghan, Peter, 71,
Kelly, Charles Aliaga, 136,
Kelly, Deirdre, 28, 99, 170,
Kelly, John, 121,

Kenny, Mr. Justice John, 94,
Kenny Report, 94,
Kenure Park, 73,
Kevin Street, Lower, 38, 41, 52,
Kevin Street Garda Station, 55,
Kilbarrack 101,
Kildare, 81, 96,
Kilkenny, 155,
Killiney, 95,
Killiney Golf Club, 95,
Kilnamanagh, 87, 88,
Kimmage, 45, 66,
King John's Castle, 156,
Kingstown, 57,
Kinsale, 76,
Kirwin's Lane, 153,
Kleihues, Josef Paul, 148,
Kreuzberg, 148, 149,
Krier, Rob, 148,

Lacey, Bill, 142,
La Defence, 150,
Larkin Unemployed Centre, 169,
Langan, Pat, 23, 30, 41, 43, 44, 104, 105, 121, 146,
Laois-Offaly, 89,
Lambert, Anthony, 88, 89, 90, 95,
Lardner, Mr. Justice, 112,
La Touche Bank, 115,
Laurence Street, 112,
Laurie, Fraser, 151,
Lavitt's Quay, 154,
Lawlor, Liam, 81, 85, 86,
Law Society, 113, 145,
Ledbetter, Peter, 103,
Lee, River, 132,
Leeson Street, Lower, 147,
Leeson Street Residents Association, Upper, 169,
Legion of Mary, 103,
Leinster House, 22,
Leixlip, 96,
Leonard's Corner, 46,
Liberties, The, 45, 48, 122, 126, 137, 138,
Liffey, 57, 59, 65, 105,
Liffey Quays, 24, 59, 60, 97, 126, 140, 144, 147, 165,
Liffey Street, 67,
Liffey Valley, 86,
Limerick, 82, 140, 155,
Linders, 142, 143, 147,
Lisbon, 27,
Liverpool, 27, 117,
Living City Group, 28, 99, 166,
London, 97, 118, 139,
London School of Economics, 33,
Lord Edward Street, 51,
Lord Mayor, 131, 165,
Loreto North Great Georges St., 118,
Los Angeles, 170,
Louis XIV, 150,
Louth Archaeological Society, 112,
Louvre, 150,

INDEX

Lucan, 76, 79, 83, 84, 85, 97, 161,
Lucey, Sean, 90,
Lumley, Ian, 21, 109, 113, 143, 165,
LUTS, 132,

M25, 97,
Maher, Joan, 85,
Malachy, High King of Ireland, 28,
Malahide Estate, 95,
Malahide Road, 74, 80,
Malone, Patrick, 89,
Malton's prints, James, 21, 115,
Manchester, 70, 170,
Manifesto for the City, 69, 82, 117, 118,
   122, 129, 156, 159, 163, 170,
Mansion House, 18, 171,
Marine School, 21,
Marlborough Street, 51,
Mater Hospital, 108, 109, 110,
M.H. (Mater Hospital) Pools, 109,
Meath, 81, 88,
Meath Hospital, 117,
Meath Street, 16, 34, 155,
Medieval City, 138, 139, 144,
Meehan, Paddy, 45, 48, 150,
Mercer's Hospital, 113, 117,
Mercer, Mary, 114,
Merchant City, 151, 152,
Merchants Quay, 154,
Merrion Gates, 56,
Merrion Road, 56, 58,
Merrion Strand, 56, 58
Merrion Street, 159,
Merrion Square, 113,
Mespil Ltd., 108,
Methodist Church, Greyfriars, 155,
Middle Street, 153,
Millennium, The, 22, 27, 28, 29, 47, 113,
   123, 130, 171,
Millennium Garden, 132,
Mishan, Prof E.J., 33,
Mitterrand, President Francois, 150,
Mogridge, Dr. Martin, 48,
Molloy, Daniel, 88, 89,
Molly Bloom's Pub, 104,
Mooney, Mary, 45, 47,
Morrissey, Paddy, 135,
Mount Street, Lower, 121, 136,
Mount Street, Upper, 113,
Mountgorry, 81, 87,
Mountjoy Square, 22, 123, 140,
Mountjoy Street, 22,
Mount Argus, 66,
Muldowney, John, 135,
Mulhall, Tony, 134, 135,
Mulhhuddert, 88,
Mumford, Lewis, 29, 125,
Municipal Gallery, 21,
Murnaghan, George, 90,
Murphy and Gunn, 95,

Murray O Laoire, 155,

McAnthony, Joe, 80,
McCarron, Gay, 133, 134,
McCarthy, Mr. Justice Niall, 93,
McCullough, Joe, 114,
McDonagh Site Eyre Sq., 153,
McDonald, Joe, 44,
McDonnell, Pat, 36, 147,
MacEoin, Uinseann, 29, 79, 97,
MacGabhann, Georoid, 108, 109,
McHugh Joe, 132,
McInerneys, 139, 145,
Mackenzie, Iain, 151,
MacLaran, Dr. Andrew, 60, 61,
Maclennan, Duncan, 150,
McLuhan, Marshall, 33,
McMahon, Des, 136,
McMahon, Larry, 81,
McMonagle, Maurice, 39,
McNamera, Shelley, 129,

Napoleon III, 150
National Association of Building Co-Operatives
   NABCO 161,
National Botonic Gardens, 20, 24, 165, 169,
National Development Plan, 69, see also Appendix Four.
National Heritage Council, 136,
National Lottery, 166,
Navan Road, 52,
Neilstown, 85,
Nelson Street, 109,
New Street, 40, 43, 46, 47, 51, 52, 62, 70,
New York Times, 21, 43,
Nicholas Street, 46, 132,
Nora Shortt v Dublin Co. Council, 91,
Norris, Senator David, 106, 107, 129,
North Circular Rd., 16, 100, 140,
North Earls Street, 131,
North Great George's Street Preservation Society, 106,
North King Street, 23, 36, 37, 51, 52, 53, 56,
North Wall, 59,

O'Casey, Sean, 16, 18,
O'Connell Street, 27, 35, 51, 52, 137, 144,
O'Connell Bridge, 67,
O'Connell Monument, 131,
O'Connor, David, 144,
O'Doherty, Edward, 112,
O'Donnell, John, 154,
O'Donnell, Liam, 100,
O'Dowd, Fergus, 112,
O'Faolain, Nuala, 34, 96,
O'Halloran, Brian, and Associates, 114,
O'Halloran, Michael, 47,
OhUiginn, Padraig O, 159,
O'Kennedy, Michael, Minister for Agriculture, 166.
O'Reilly, Christine, 24,
ORiain, Gearoid, 158,
O'Rourke, Horace Tennyson, 135,

INDEX

Observer magazine, 20,
Office of Public Works, 22, 164, 166, 168,
Ontario, 33,
Ormonde Quay, 67, 68, 128.

Palace of St. Sepulchre, 55,
Palmerstown, 86, 97,
Palm House, 24, 169,
Paris, 68, 99, 149, 150,
Parliament Inn, 38,
Parliament Street, 38, 145,
Parnell, 85,
Parnell Square, 22,
Parnell Street, 28, 30, 34, 35, 51, 52, 53, 56, 64, 137, 145,
Patrick, Jim, 151,
Patrick Dun's, Sir, 117,
Patrick Street, 40, 43, 44, 46, 47, 51, 52, 62, 70, 143, 144,
Paul, John, 113,
Paul Street, 135, 154,
Peace Garden, 132,
Pearse Street, 24,
Pearse Station, 60,
Pembroke, 162,
Penrice's Tower, 153,
Phoenix Park, 22, 59, 145,
Pimlico, 53,
Plan Magazine, 96,
Planning Acts, 28, 87, 91, 92, 93, 95, 110, 126,
   141, 143, 162, 163,
Planning Compensation Bill, 92, 94
Planning Department, 133,
Planning Officer, 133,
Plantation site, 88,
Pleanail, 134, 144,
Port Access Route, 53, 63, 65,
Portabello Road, 145,
Post, An, 76,
Potato Market, 156,
Power Securities, 90, 102,
Power, Robin, 142,
Powder Tower, 115,
Prendergast, John, 18, 67, 133,
Progressive Democrats, 47, 159,

Queen Maeve's Bridge, 59,
Queens Street, 53, 59, 104, 135,
Quinlan Paddy, 133,

Ranelagh, 16,
Rathfarham, 161,
Rathmines, 160, 162,
Reading University, 27,
Reddy, Tony, 8, 141,
Redmill, John, 113,
Redmond, George, 98,
Redmonds Hill, 38, 41,
Regent's Park, 164,
Reid McHugh & Partners, 52, 57, 68, 115,
Rent Restrictions Act, 101,
RESCUE, 40,

Revenue building, 115,
Reynolds, Albert, Minister & TD, 107, 129,
Reynolds, Michael, 142,
Richmond Hospital, 117,
Ringsend, 123, 126,
Riversdale, 86,
Rising, 1916, 134,
Roche, John, 153,
Rocheshill, 95,
Rock Rd, 56,
Rogers, Richard, 164,
Rogerson's Quay, Sir John, 21,
Rome, 20,
Rossi, Aldo, 148,
Royal Canal, 15, 59, 140,
Royal College Of Surgeons, 113, 114,
Royal Institute of the Architects of Ireland,
   17, 28, 40, 134, 141, 160, 164, 169, 171
RIAI's Millennium Conference, 171, see Appendix Three.
RTE, 18, 165,
Rush, 73,
Rutland Street Upper, 17,
Ryders Row, 56,
Ryde International, 108,

St. Augustine Street, 153,
St. Andrews School, 118,
St. Audeon's Park, 132,
St. Georges Church, 111, 121,
St. Helen's, 56,
St. John's Square, 155,
St. Jude's, Inchicore, 121,
St. Mary's, Mary St., 120,
St. Nicholas and St. Luke's, 120,
St. Patrick's Cathedral, 46, 48, 144,
St. Paul's, Arran Quay, 147,
St. Peters, Aungier St., 120,
St. Stephens Green, 20, 32, 36, 67, 101, 102, 114, 131, 137,
St. Vincents Hospital on the Green, 117,
Sandymount Strand, 56, 58,
Sarsfield Quay, 105,
Scotland, 152,
Scottish Development Agency, 150, 151,
Scott Tallon Walker, 24,
Scudds, Colin, 31,
Sean McDermott Street, 154,
Seapoint, 123,
Shaffrey, Patrick, 76,
Shandon, 154,
Shannon Development, 155,
Sheeran, Gerard, 155,
Sheriff Street Flats, 139,
Ship Street Barracks, 115,
Shoemaker's Tower, 153,
Sick and Indigent Roomkeepers Society, 132,
Singleton House, 112,
Slattery, David, 114,
Smithfield, 24, 138, 139, 142, 144, 145, 147,
Society of Chartered Surveyors, 99, 102, 119, 126,
South Circular Rd., 18,

INDEX

South City markets, 119,
South Finglas, 74,
South Great Georges Street, 145,
South Inner City Community Development Asociation,138,
South Kings St., 20,114,
South Parish, 154,
South Terr., 154,
South William Street, 145,
Special Amenity Area Order, SAAO, 86,
Special Criminal Court, 24,
Spring, Dick, 81, 89, 90,
Spring Garden Alley, 155,
Stack C, 139,
Stafford, Jim, 108,
State Apartments, 114, 115
Steeven's Hospital, Dr., 117,
Stephenson, Sam, 113,
Sterling, James, 148,
STERN, (Careful Urban Renewal Co. Ltd.), 149,
Stillorgan Road, 52, 56,
Stockholm, 170,
Stokes Kennedy Crowley, 52, 57, 68, 115,
Store St. Garda Station, 17,
Strand Road, 58,
Strudwick, Roy, 108,
Students Against The Destruction of Dublin, SADD,
   45, 109, 143,
Sullivan, Michael, 71,
Sullivan's Quay, 154,
Summerhill, 17,
Sunday Independent, 27, 80, 81, 93,
Supreme Court, 87, 91, 110,
Swords, 80, 81,
Synge Street, 130.

Taheny, Stephanie, 155.
Taisce, An, 21, 22, 24, 26, 28, 89, 107, 108, 109, 114,
   132, 136, 138, 142, 143, 154, 164, 165, 166,
Taj Mahal, 27,
Talbot Street, 145,
Tallaght, 50, 53, 60, 65, 66, 74, 75, 76, 78, 79, 83,
   84, 87, 91, 140, 161, 162,
Taoiseach's Department, 22, 159,
Tara Street, 22, 65,
Temple Bar, 48, 50, 67, 126, 127, 128, 141, 144, 151,
Temple Bar Study Group, 68,
Temple Bar Development Council, 127,
Temple Street Hospital, 118, 133,
Templeogue, 62,
Tenement Rehabilitation Programme, 152,
The Dead, 59,
Tholsel, 21,
Thomas Court, 53,
Thomas Street Library, 21,
Thursfield, Peter, 37,
Times, London, 164,
Tobin, Liam, 98,
Toibin, Colm, 27,
Toronto, 33,
Transport Consultative Commission, 61, 62, 63,

Transportation Centre, 127,
Treasury building, 115,
Trinity College, 24, 35, 60, 61, 144,
Turner, Richard, 165,
Turner Glasshouses, 166,
Tyneside, 97,

UCD, University College Dublin, 16, 17, 26, 145,
UCG, University College Galway, 153,
Ulysses, 54,
United Kingdom, 152,
University College of London, 48,
Upper Merrion Street , 22,
Urban Renewal Act 1986, 128,
Urban Renewal Area NO. 3, 138,
U.S.A., 130,140,
Ushers island, 25, 53, 59,
Ushers Quay, 59,

VEC, 22
Venice, 20,
Vicar Street, 29,
Viking Exhibition Centre Dublin, 127,
Viking & Medieval area, 126,
Viking Museum, Roskilde, 126,
Viscount Securities V Dublin Co. Council, 91,

Walsh, Sean, 81, 85,
Waterford, 82, 120, 134, 140, 155,
Watkins, Jameson & Pim, 42,
Watts, Dr. Bill, 24,
Wellington Quay, 67,
Wesley College, 118,
West Clare Railway, 69,
Western Parkway, 59,
Westland Row, 24, 60
West Finglas, 29,
West Germany, 140,
Westmoreland Street, 22, 35,
Wexford, 140,
Whitehall, 56,
White House Bar, The, 43,
Wide Streets Commission, 35, 127, 164,
Wilde, Oscar, 24,
Wilson, John TD, 50,
Winetavern Street, 120, 166,
Wolf Tone, 120,
Wood Quay, 26, 48, 120, 136, 166, 168,
Wright, Myles, 79, 81,

XJS Investments v Dun Laoghaire Corporation, 93, 95,

YMCA, 120,
York, 126,
York University, 134, 135,